The Open University

Humanities: A Foundation Course   **Units 29 — 36**

Industrialisation and Culture

Unit 31   THE DEBATE ON INDUSTRIALISATION

Prepared by Christopher Harvie, Graham Holderness and Graham Martin for the Arts Foundation Course Team

THE OPEN UNIVERSITY PRESS

The Open University Press
Walton Hall Bletchley Bucks

First published 1971. Reprinted 1973
Copyright © 1971 The Open University

Designed by the Media Development Group of The Open University

Printed in Great Britain by
EYRE AND SPOTTISWOODE LIMITED
AT GROSVENOR PRESS PORTSMOUTH

SBN 335 00524 1

Open University courses provide a method of study for independent learners through
an integrated teaching system, including textual material, radio and television programmes
and short residential courses. This text is one of a series that makes up the correspondence
element of the Arts Foundation Course.

For general availability of supporting material referred to in this text, please write to the
Director of Marketing, The Open University, Walton Hall, Bletchley, Bucks.

Further information on Open University courses may be obtained from the Admissions
Office, The Open University, P.O. Box 48, Bletchley, Bucks.

THE DEBATE ON INDUSTRIALISATION

CONTENTS

INTRODUCTION

The general aim of this unit is to study the debate on the gains and losses of industrialisation as it was carried on in the nineteenth century, between the protagonists and critics of the modern industrial state.

The debate was one about culture and attitudes to life, tradition, and individual values. The problems at issue were created by the industrialisation process discussed in Units 29–30, but the analysis and debate were carried on not only in political but in artistic and literary terms. Some analyses of the industrial experience were essentially rationalisations of their own situations by the various groups which took part in it; others resulted from the perceptions of individual commentators being implanted in the contemporary consciousness. Both were constantly interrelated, and from both came prescriptions for the future.

Disentangling such relationships, and evaluating the contribution to the debate of the critics of industrialism in a literary as well as a political sense, is a complex process, but also a valid field for inter-disciplinary study. So in this unit we look first at the way in which the industrial experience was coped with politically and socially by the groups which participated in it, and end by examining the *political* importance in this context of the literary critics of industrialism. In the second part of the unit (sections 4–9) we will examine the arguments, language and imagery of the critics themselves, assessing how they contributed to the force of their criticism, and in their turn, to their relevance to subsequent literary activity.

While reading through this unit you should have Units 29–30 and the course anthology *Industrialisation and Culture* by you, since frequent reference will be made to them throughout. There is no television broadcast associated with this unit, but two radio broadcasts: Dr. Brian Harrison discusses Victorian social investigators in *Finding Out How the Other Half Lives*, this is shared with Unit 30,

anthology:
Industrialisation and Culture
broadcasts

the relevant supplement being distributed to students with that unit; and, in the week of Unit 32, Professor Ian Gregor on *The Victorian Social Critics*; the supplement to that broadcast is distributed with this unit and should be looked at beforehand.

Of the books on the Recommended Reading list Raymond Williams' *Culture and Society* is invaluable as a study of the British literary tradition of social criticism from the French Revolution to the mid-twentieth century. recommended books

This is unavoidably a lengthy and complex unit. For reasons of space we ask you to reply to most of the questions in the margin, but you may prefer to use a separate notebook. Whatever you do, make sure your answer and the text are kept together. You may also find it useful to keep a sheet of card or paper by you to 'mask' specimen answers.

An assignment (tutor-marked) for Units 29–31 is included with this unit. It consists of four questions, one for each part of 29–30 and one for 31. Do not attempt it, however, until you have been through Unit 31. assignment

THE DEBATE ON INDUSTRIALISATION

Synopsis of sections:

SECTION 1   In which we study the costs and benefits of the industrial experience, the way in which contemporary commentators related to it, and the range of their reactions.

SECTION 2   We discuss the failure of individualism – the motor of industrialisation – to cope with the problems of the mass society it created, and the emergence of a modified liberalism which rejected belief in an automatic, unfettered, and beneficial 'progress' in favour of a greater concern with individual values and a greater willingness to accept state intervention to secure these.

SECTION 3   We discuss the development of the politics of the working class in the society created by capitalist industry, how it managed at once to coexist with capitalism yet develop its own institutions and class-consciousness. We end by looking at the growth of the socialist movement in Britain and the contribution of literary and artistic critics to the development of an anti-capitalist political ideology.

SECTION 4   We study the 'religious' basis of British social criticism which distinguishes it from the 'scientific socialist' approach of the continent.

SECTION 5   We study Thomas Carlyle's reinterpretation of Christianity in secular terms, and his application of its moral imperatives and imagery to the criticism of the nineteenth-century industrial state.

SECTION 6 We study the social critics' attitude to man and the machine, and their use of the metaphor of the machine as the antithesis of the 'religious' and the humane.

SECTION 7 Taking as an example George Eliot and her native Midlands, we discuss the reaction of a provincial intellectual to social change within a familiar environment.

SECTION 8 We discuss the responses of Thomas Hardy and D. H. Lawrence to the intrusion of the methods and values of industrialism into rural society.

SECTION 9 Using Barbara's dialogue with Undershaft in Bernard Shaw's *Major Barbara*, we conclude our study by contrasting the religious criteria, language and imagery of nineteenth-century social commentators with the rationalist language of pragmatic social amelioration as vehicles for social criticism.

Sections 1–4 were written by Christopher Harvie, 5–9 by Graham Holderness, with the collaboration of Graham Martin.

PROPHETS AND SCEPTICS IN CONTEXT

In this unit we will be discussing writers who concerned themselves with the impact of industrialisation on the quality of individual and social life. You have most likely come away from Units 29 and 30 with the feeling that industrialisation entailed costs as well as benefits: this reaction was shared by people alive at the time of the changes. Whether in general they approved or disapproved of them, they never forgot that the consequences of industrialism were a subject of continuous debate.

In discussing this debate, we have chosen first of all to study the way in which the costs and benefits of industrialisation became matters of public debate, who conducted the debate, and who it was aimed at. Then we will concentrate on certain significant critical figures who acted as a bridge between social thinking and action and the creative arts, including Matthew Arnold, Thomas Carlyle and John Ruskin.

At this early stage we might face a difficult problem of evaluation: we must be very careful to distinguish between political evaluations of writers' work (e.g. in terms of actual effectiveness) and literary evaluations. Over-emphasis on either side could distort our appreciation of the achievement of the writers in question.

Distinguishing between political and literary criteria in estimating the contribution of a man like, say, Carlyle, is a very complicated matter. For instance, the high value placed by a modern literary commentator on a Victorian critical writer might lead him to credit him with political importance as well – an importance which a study of the politics of the period might not bear out. Similarly, historical study which confined itself to an analysis, say, of political behaviour at elections might relegate the ideological element in politics – and consequently the influence of individual thinkers – to a footnote, or ignore it completely. We propose to tackle this problem by looking at the context in which these social critics wrote, the contemporary trend in ideology and political actuality, and then at the arguments of the critics themselves, and the language they used to formulate them.

Let us look first of all at what the problems were which constituted the agenda of the debate, at how social commentators related to them, and at the range of opinions they expressed.

EXERCISE

In the last two units we have seen several of the benefits of industrialisation and also examples of the sort of price that had to be paid for them. So I want you to go through these and, in the boxes below, note down the 'benefits' and 'costs' of the aspect of industrialisation discussed in each section.

For example, let's take section 2.1

Benefits	Costs
2.1 New forms of commercial organisation enable better engineered roads and water communications systems.	But commercial organisation means that local people's 'rights' are lessened, and the emphasis changed to cash payment.

The notes you make don't have to be elaborate. You may find that certain sections yield only one point for or against, or a multitude of small points that don't seem significant enough to take down. Don't worry, most of the sections contain one fairly easily identifiable point that you've probably already noticed.

Benefits	Costs
1.1	
1.2 Total employment numbers rise. exports up - bal of payments ↓ railways boom	
1.3 imps. in ship iron prod + cotton imports up	
1.4 improvements in ships & locos?	
1.5	~~but~~ specialisation
1.6	

Benefits	Costs
2.1	
2.2	
2.3	
2.4	
2.5	

Benefits	Costs
3.1	
3.2	
3.3	

3·4	
3·5	
3.6	

SPECIMEN ANSWER

	Benefits	Costs
1.1		
1.2	Employment figures are evidence of great increase in manufactures and services.	
1.3	Industrial growth stimulates technical innovation.	
1.4	Technical innovation and engineering give man's imagination and intellect scope.	
1.5		The function of the engineer itself is divided into a number of narrow specialisms. Heavy investment in equipment can lead to a reluctance to innovate and eventual obsolescence.
1.6		Labour on the railways is both divided by specialisations and harshly disciplined both by management and the equipment it handles.

Benefits	Costs
2.1 New forms of commercial organisation enable better engineered roads and water communication systems.	But commercial organisation means that the emphasis is changed to cash payment, and local people's 'rights' are lessened.
2.2 As above.	
2.3 The machinery for funding major programmes of investment like railways (the joint-stock company) is set up.	This strengthens the speculator and those who live on unearned income.
2.4 New forms of management for enterprises like railways have to be evolved.	The morality of commerce is not above reproach.
2.5 Competition between lines improves the services offered.	The tendency of railway owners is seen to be towards amalgamation and monopoly. Competition promotes wasteful investment. Eventually government has to intervene.

Benefits	Costs
3.1 Industry expands the commerce of Glasgow.	
3.2 Transport improvement plays an important role in this.	
3.3 Local natural resources and expertise combine to make an area specialise in one type of manufacture.	The drawback to this is that skills and equipment can become obsolete. Labour relations in the works are also strained.
3.4 Most of us are today dependent on the services and facilities which the modern city, serving an extensive region, provides for us. This has led to an increased variety in our lives.	

3.5 Public intervention helps secure the benefits of mechanised transport to the community.	The benefits of city life are only gradually made available to the majority of the city's inhabitants. Technology, in fact, depresses rather than elevates their standard of life, until public bodies intervene.
3.6 Most of the commodities, goods and services we take for granted today are brought to us through a combination of industrialised production, mechanised transport, and the mass market.	A mass market tends to make for an absence of individuality.

DISCUSSION

Let's tidy this collection of pros and cons up:

On the credit side we have:

(a) *expansion* of output, population, cities, service industries (1.2, 3.1, 3.6);

(b) *innovation* in technical and economic terms (1.3, 1.4, 2.1, 2.2, 2.3, 2.4, 3.2);

(c) *competitiveness* improving the quality of goods and services offered (2.5);

(d) ultimately a measure of *democratic control* of the machinery of the industrial state, to secure to all classes the benefit of industrial organisation (2.5, 3.5).

On the debit side:

(a) *instability* – the need for continual adjustments to cope with a rapidly changing technology which rendered redundant traditional skills and older equipment (1.5, 3.3);

(b) *over-specialisation* which made work monotonous, adaptation to new circumstances difficult (1.5, 3.3);

(c) *wasteful competition and lack of planning* which resulted from 'laissez-faire' and made the task of coping with industrial society's problems more difficult (2.5, 3.5);

(d) *harsh work-discipline* imposed on the worker by the machines he worked with and condoned by management (1.6);

(e) *exploitation* both of the worker and the consumer by businessmen determined on maximising their profits and the possessors of unearned incomes through shares (2.1, 2.2, 2.3, 2.4);

(f) *loss of individual identity* in a society geared to a mass-market (3.6);

(g) *class division* through the ownership of the means of production and distribution by a small, wealthy, minority (3.3, 3.5).

11

Taken together, these give us an 'agenda' of the main matters at issue in a discussion of the impact of industrialisation on society, which will recur frequently during the rest of this unit.

EXERCISE

Now let us look at how the social commentators we will be studying related to industrial society with all its stresses and strains. An obvious line of approach is through their social status and occupations. So, given the common social concern of the contributors to section H of *Industrialisation and Culture* (and bearing in mind that the conclusions they came to differed considerably), I want you to look at the occupations and major intellectual activities – that is, besides social criticism – of some of them. Note down, in the boxes provided, how these might have led them to concern themselves with social questions (use the biographical details preceding each extract):

Goldwin Smith

> Intellectually interested in socialism ..
> Prof of Mod. Hist.

Karl Marx

> Journalist writer polit
> polit. activities find voice in writings

Matthew Arnold

> as school inspector would be concerned with
> educ.

Augustus Welby Northmore Pugin

> .. archit. nat. interested in housing
> Romantic

William Morris

> Romantic – concerned with politics.

How would you sum up the relations of their occupations to their social criticism?

> all intell. int. in socialism

SPECIMEN ANSWERS

Goldwin Smith

> the writing of history is a social function and involves the expression of judgements about society; as does the reform of the educational system

Karl Marx

> as historian see Goldwin Smith; a political activist cannot avoid being involved in making social judgements

Matthew Arnold

> as educationalist see Goldwin Smith; as a creative artist and more importantly as a critic, must be concerned with the relationship between the arts and society

Augustus Welby Northmore Pugin

> the architect as a creative artist has close relations with social requirements for his skills

William Morris

> as designer, see Pugin; as activist, see Karl Marx

GENERAL SUMMING UP

> In general, most of these occupations seem in part reflective and analytical ones, distanced to some extent from actual involvement in the business of production.

DISCUSSION

This exercise was intended to make two general points: that the most influential nineteenth-century social commentators came from an environment where a traditional intellectual activity, that of historian or literary critic or whatever, was inevitably engaged in a dialogue with the effects of industrial and social change; and that such an environment was distanced to some extent from the actual business of industrial organisation.

These factors meant that social commentators were acutely aware of the cultural implications of change, and that they were distant enough from it to take a comprehensive view (although it could also be argued that this distance did little but decrease their knowledge of what was going on).

EXERCISE

Now I want you to look at six of the extracts from *Industrialisation and Culture*, and grade them in order of what you think is their degree of hostility towards industrial society.

13

Three of the extracts are from writers who, if not altogether enthusiastic about the changes, by and large accepted them:

H4   Goldwin Smith: *The Laws of Political Economy*
H6   John Stuart Mill: *The Peril of Uniformity*
H7   Matthew Arnold: *Culture and Machinery*

Three are from more resolute critics:

H9   Thomas Carlyle: *Hudson's Statue*
H10   A. W. N. Pugin: *Contrasted Towns*
H12   William Morris: *How I became a Socialist*

I want you to enter your decisions in the boxes 1–6 putting the title of the extract into the top section, and in the bottom section jot down briefly the reasons for your choice.

Most enthusiastic

1. *H4*
2. *H6*
3. *H7*
4. *H12*
5. *H10*
6. *H9*

Least enthusiastic

SPECIMEN ANSWERS

My own order would be:

Most enthusiastic

1. Goldwin Smith

   the system of individualist economics is seen as a God-given boon, operating under its own infallible laws

2. John Stuart Mill

   industrial progress and the resulting egalitarian society is accepted as inevitable but he has doubts about its repercussions on individuals and suspects that it will impose uniformity of thought and action

3. Thomas Carlyle

   progress – the building of railways and so on is inevitable, but has been attended with a lowering of standards of conduct on the part of the public and an absence of foresight and concern for the implications of such developments

4. William Morris

   is disposed to detest 'civilisation' and look back to an older society, but realises that out of nineteenth-century industrial society has come the organised working class as the agent which will destroy industrial capitalism

5. Matthew Arnold

   argues that no correlation can be made between the material wealth of an age and its cultural achievement, and contrasts the Victorian age unfavourably with the Elizabethan

6. Augustus Welby Northmore Pugin

   contrasts the ugliness of a contemporary town with the beauty and grace it had possessed (or he thought it had possessed) during the Middle Ages

DISCUSSION

Now, this is my own interpretation of these extracts, and yours may have differed. In particular, you may have reversed the order of Carlyle and Arnold, although I think in this instance the extract makes Carlyle look marginally more favourable to industrialisation than Arnold. Remember, however, that I graded these by reference to the extracts themselves, not to any further information I had on the authors. The order in *Industrialisation and Culture* is, taking their careers and other writings into account, a more accurate assessment of where they stood in relation to industrialisation. Matthew Arnold was, as a government inspector of schools, more disposed to put his faith in the ability of nineteenth-century democratic government to remedy the evils of a materialistic society than the extract would indicate. Pugin, for all his mediaeval yearnings, was eager to apply the gothic style to modern things like railway bridges and stations, and William Morris, for all his hopes of a coming revolution of the industrial working class, excluded all the machinery of the nineteenth century from his socialist Utopia in *News from Nowhere*.

But in general we can assume that a dividing line can be detected between those thinkers who were involved in parliamentary politics and government activity, and were thus accustomed to use the prevailing liberal ideology as a framework for their thought; and those who drew their criteria for social criticism from religious or artistic sources. It is among these that we find industrialisation's most resolute critics.

These three exercises have, I hope, introduced you to:

1. The problems which the debate on industrialisation dealt with.

2. The sort of professional and intellectual environment from which nineteenth-century social commentators tended to come.

3. The range of opinions voiced during the debate, and the general distinction between the 'marginal' criticisms made by those close to the political mainstream and the more fundamental disquiet of creative artists.

Now these generalisations are very wide ones, but they provide us with a provisional framework for further analysis. So I think it's worth while to start with mainstream politics and their response to the problems of industrialisation, and work out how this affected the ruling ideology of those close to government, the British liberals.

SECTION 2

LIBERAL INDIVIDUALISM AND ITS CRITICS

In the 1860s, when Goldwin Smith, James Bryce, John Stuart Mill and Matthew Arnold were writing or had just written the works, extracts from which you will find in section H of *Industrialisation and Culture*, the influence of liberal individualism as a political ideology had reached its zenith. What in essence this ideology was you can find out by reading through these extracts and also Karl Marx's description of 'The Manchester Party' (*Industrialisation and Culture* H2).

EXERCISE

In particular, look at the passage from Goldwin Smith (H4). If you want, make a precis of what appears to you to be his argument. In the margin I want you to note down, very briefly, what you imagine his attitude would be to the degree of government intervention in the economy that we have today.

ANSWER IN MARGIN

SPECIMEN ANSWER

Precis
In economic dealings one should be guided neither by notions of duty nor by sympathy for any of the parties concerned; economic laws are natural laws, which depend on the self-interest of the individual being the standard of conduct. Left to themselves, they will work smoothly and ensure an equitable distribution of resources.

Smith would certainly not have approved of government intervention in the economy, as this would have the effect of imposing a distortion on the operations of the market, and so throwing the whole pattern of relationships out of joint.

DISCUSSION

If you compare Smith's views with the programme of the Manchester men described by Karl Marx, you will see how closely his thumbnail economic analysis fits into their political ideas. He was in fact the favourite academic of Richard Cobden and John Bright, the leaders of the businessmen radicals in parliament.

Although individualist radicals of the stamp of Cobden, Bright and Smith were always in a minority in a parliament still dominated by the landed interest, their ideas of Free Trade abroad (involving the cutting of protective tariffs) and a minimal role for the government in domestic policy, were the main current of opinion in the major governmental institutions of mid-Victorian Britain. They had agitated for and benefited by the Reform Act of 1832, which enfranchised the propertied classes of the new industrial areas of Britain. Later they secured an ultimately decisive victory over the landed interest when they obtained almost simultaneously, in 1846–7, the repeal of the duties which were charged on otherwise cheap imports of foreign corn to make them more expensive than the home product, and the collapse of the Tory party, riven by a division between its traditional landed supporters and men of industrial and mercantile property like Sir Robert Peel and W. E. Gladstone who wanted to come to terms with the new age and adopt the economic policies associated with liberalism. Thereafter, for nearly thirty years, the Tories were almost permanently in opposition, conferring on themselves, with some pride, the title of 'the stupid party', and allowing themselves to be led by a man whom most of Victorian society considered an irresponsible adventurer, Benjamin Disraeli. The Liberals, led by the aristocratic Whigs but pushed from behind by the radicals, held the stage.

By the middle of the 1860s another showdown was imminent. Changes in population had made the boundaries of constituencies created in 1832 obsolete, and perpetuated the grotesque over-representation of small towns like Chippenham in Wiltshire, whose 600 voters sent the same number of M.P.s to Westminster as the city of Manchester (population 339,000). The radicals agitated for a new reform bill, involving redistribution and the granting of the franchise to the urban workmen, or at least the more respectable among them, on the grounds that if they were not incorporated into the political institutions of the nation, they might reinforce their own – the growing trade unions and co-operatives – and become a state within a state.

The radicals put pressure on the Whigs to grant a further measure of reform. The American Civil War, between 1862 and 1865, further polarised British society as the landed interest tended to identify with what they considered the 'chivalry' of the South, and while working men and middle-class radicals sided with the 'democratic' North. Agitation increased by the middle of the 1860s, mass demonstrations took place in major towns, and in the summer of 1866 a Reform crowd actually stormed Hyde Park, then a preserve of the 'quality' of London, after a revolt by conservative Liberals in parliament had halted the Liberal government's reform bill. Eventually Disraeli's Conservative ministry of 1867–8 under continual pressure from radical Liberals passed a measure enfranchising all urban householders and redistributing constituencies. In 1884 the franchise was further extended to all householders in county constituencies, although the first women were not enfranchised until 1918, and the principle of 'one man one vote' was not statutorily enacted until 1948.

In 1867–8 Britain took an important step towards parliamentary democracy. Now it might appear that this would be welcomed by liberals, indeed, if you read the passage by James Bryce in *Industrialisation and Culture* it appears virtually an inevitable step. Yet most of the disquiet voiced at the time came from men who considered themselves liberals like John Stuart Mill and Matthew Arnold, and Thomas Carlyle, no Liberal but, as we shall see, a seminal influence in radical social criticism in the nineteenth century, damned everyone concerned with, as he put it, 'shooting Niagara'.

As the reform agitation went on, there was a steady output of tracts, magazine articles, and books by intellectuals, mainly Liberals, about the likely nature and consequences of democratic government. Mill's *On Liberty* was followed by his *Representative Government* in 1863. James Bryce, Goldwin Smith, and a dozen or so other radical Oxford and Cambridge dons produced two volumes of *Essays on Reform* in 1867, in which year was also published George Eliot's *Felix Holt, The Radical*, and a couple of years later came Matthew Arnold's *Culture and Anarchy*. But none of these was unqualified in its enthusiasm for the course of democratic individualism upheld by the parliamentary radicals, although their authors included able and sincere liberals. What caused this?

In *Culture and Anarchy* (*Industrialisation and Culture* H7) you have one British liberal intellectual's view of the implications of industrialised society and its politics in the 1860s. I want you to compare it with this extract from another essay on democracy, industrialisation and culture, written by the American poet, Walt Whitman, two years after Arnold, in 1871, called *Democratic Vistas*.

> Did you, too, O friend, suppose democracy was only for elections, for politics, and for a party name? I say democracy is only of use there that it may pass on and come to its flower and fruits in manners, in the highest forms of interaction between men, and their beliefs – in religion, literature, colleges, and schools – democracy in all public and private life, and in the army and navy. I have intimated that, as a paramount scheme, it has yet few or no full realizers and believers. I do not see, either, that it owes any serious thanks to noted propagandists or champions, or has been essentially help'd, though often harm'd, by them. It has been and is carried on by all the moral forces, and by trade, finance, machinery, intercommunications, and, in fact, by all the developments of history, and can no more be stopp'd than the tides, or the earth in its orbit. Doubtless, also, it resides crude and latent, well down in the hearts of the fair average of the American-born people, mainly in the agricultural regions. But it is not yet, there or anywhere, the fully-receiv'd, the fervid, the absolute faith.
>
> I submit, therefore, that the fruition of democracy, on aught like a grand scale, resides altogether in the future. As, under any profound and comprehensive view of the gorgeous-composite feudal world, we see in it, through the long ages and cycles of ages, the results of a deep, integral, human and divine principle, or fountain, from which issued laws, ecclesia, manners, institutes, costumes, personalities, poems, (hitherto unequall'd,) faithfully partaking of their source, and indeed only arising either to betoken it, or to furnish parts of that varied-flowing display, whose centre was one and absolute – so, long ages hence, shall the due historian or critic make at least an equal retrospect, an equal history for the democratic principle. It too must be adorn'd, credited with its results – then, when it, with imperial power, through amplest time, has dominated mankind – has been the source and test of all the moral, esthetic, social, political, and religious expressions and institutes of the civilized world – has begotten them in spirit and in form, and has carried them to its own unprecedented heights – has had, (it is possible,) monastics and ascetics, more numerous, more devout than the monks and priests of all previous creeds – has sway'd the ages with a breadth and rectitude tallying Nature's own – has fashion'd, systematized, and triumphantly finish'd and carried out, in its own interest, and with unparallel'd success, a new earth and a new man.

EXERCISE

1. What are the main differences you notice between the passage from Arnold and the passage from Whitman?
2. Can you suggest a reason for these differences?

ANSWER IN MARGIN

Fig. 1 Walt Whitman

SPECIMEN ANSWERS

> 1. The things about the culture of an industrialised state which Arnold has doubts about are to Whitman positive virtues: he sees railroads, industry and popular politics as components of a new democratic culture, valid and artistic means of self-expression in an expanding, democratic state. He has respect for the traditional culture 'the magnificent legacy of feudalism' but believes the new culture of industrialism and democracy will surpass it. Arnold's idea of cultivation is still to a great extent concerned with the preservation of the excellences of the past and the creation of a public with the intellect and taste to honour them.

> 2. Possibly a reason for Whitman's enthusiasm and Arnold's doubts is that America was still a young nation, whose institutions were still those she had acquired second-hand from Europe, whose towns and buildings were new and ever-changing. Great schemes could be carried through without disturbing the achievements of a settled order. In Britain, on the other hand, there were always traditions in art and literature, established townscapes and landscapes, whose integrity had to be respected.

DISCUSSION

What Whitman demonstrates is a confidence in the vitality of the democratic nation that Arnold lacks. He revels in the unpredictability of American invention and ingenuity, in the prospect of being surprised and bewildered by new developments. Arnold is more concerned with what or who is going to get hurt in the process.

And it's only natural that he should be. He has been accustomed to a familiar culture, written and visible, to long-established social and religious arrangements, and to a particularly charming and interesting landscape. So naturally the unpredictability of the democratic industrial state alarms him.

As our comparison between Arnold and Whitman has indicated, it was rather difficult for any British commentator to give the same sort of whole-hearted commendation to industrialisation and political democracy as his American contemporary. The past and its artifacts lay heavily on Britain, and on nowhere did they lie more heavily than on the education system. A young man, given a liberal education – in other words one devoted almost exclusively to the classics – at a mediaeval 'public school' – and then at a mediaeval university, would come away with a strong pre-disposition to look on change with suspicion. Even if, like Arnold, he accepted its inevitability, he would be concerned to protect the best of the older culture. It's interesting to note that Goldwin Smith, whose panegyric about economics you have been reading, and who was the greatest radical of his day at Oxford, was aghast when in 1865 the Great Western proposed to build its carriage works (which you visited in *Life in a Railway Factory*) there, although his father had been one of the G.W.R's first directors.

Nor was the business community immune to the attractions of the traditional life of the propertied classes in England. The Manchester manufacturers Marx sketched for the readers of the *New York Daily Tribune* seem a pretty hard-headed lot, but eventually a good many settled for a country estate for themselves, a university education and a seat in parliament for their sons. Beatrice Webb's father, for example, who had been a Manchester cotton man, eventually possessed several country houses and, lacking sons, married his seven daughters off to gentry and professional men.

This attraction towards older patterns of life meant that British justifications of progress in terms of industrial advance are somehow less convincing than those of American commentators. They tended to be written by manufacturers who thought early on that Manchester was the greatest place on earth, but later discovered the delights of the traditional life of the gentry; or by hacks simply concerned to win a dishonest penny, who could be counted on to defend everything from unpurified water supplies to child labour in factories, and figure much as part of Karl Marx's demonology of British capitalism.

Let's consider, however, a much more honest apologist for industrialisation whom we have met already, Samuel Smiles. I want you to go back and read over the passages in section 1.4 in which we discuss his treatment of George Stephenson, and then consider the passage below. What would you consider to be the flaws in his judgement of Stephenson's work?

> The poverty of his parents being such that they could not give him any, even the very simplest, education, beyond the good example of integrity and industry, he was early left to shift for himself, and compelled to be self-reliant. Having the will to learn, he soon found a way for himself. No beginning could have been more humble than his; but he persevered: he had determined to learn, and he did learn. To such a resolution as his, nothing really beneficial in life is denied. He might have said, like Sebastian Bach, 'I was

industrious; and whoever is equally sedulous will be equally successful'.

The whole secret of Mr. Stephenson's success in life was his careful improvement of time, which is the rock out of which fortunes are carved and great characters formed. He believed in genius to the extent that Buffon did when he said that 'patience is genius'; or as some other thinker put it, when he defined genius to be the power of making efforts. But he never would have it that he was a genius, or that he had done anything which other men, equally laborious and persevering as himself, could not have accomplished. He repeatedly said to the young men about him: 'Do as I have done – persevere!'

Every step of advance which he made was conquered by patient labour. When an engineman, he systematically took his engine to pieces on Saturday afternoons while the works were at a stand, for the purpose of cleaning it thoroughly, and 'gaining insight'. He thus gradually mastered the mechanism of the steam-engine, so that, when opportunity offered, he was enabled to improve it, and to make it work even when its own maker was baffled. He practically studied hydraulics in the same plodding way, when acting as plugman; and when all the local pump-doctors at Killingworth were in despair, he stepped in, and successfully applied the knowledge which he had so laboriously gained. A man of such a temper and purpose could not but succeed in life.

ANSWER IN MARGIN

SPECIMEN ANSWER

> Smiles obviously thinks that his gospel of 'self-help' is universally applicable, that every artisan has it in his power to become a Stephenson or a Telford. But even assuming everyone trained himself to the same technical standards as Stephenson, the *supply* of engineers would greatly exceed the *demand* for their services, and they would get little out of their additional qualifications. Secondly, the 'self-help' of individuals in one generation influences the chances of the next: Robert Stephenson, Isambard Kingdom Brunel and the younger Rennie, obviously got a head start because of their fathers' eminence and wealth. Thirdly, there is no necessary correlation between success in business and moral worth or even technical ingenuity. Smiles played down George Stephenson's ruthless treatment of his old patron William James and the mechanical genius of the unsuccessful Richard Trevithick.

DISCUSSION

Smiles is, as I have said, about as close as you can get to a whole-hearted believer in industrial progress, yet his argument seems hopelessly flawed. Only a man of really generous temperament at the head of a profession will help the rise of men who might prove to be his rivals, and we can scarcely imagine him trying to impede the careers of his own family. And the businessman who preached the virtues of competition on his way up is likely to feel less enthusiastic about them when he sees the possibility of a lucrative monopoly for his own enterprises.

Even in the more 'open' society of America, where men could escape from the more rigidly stratified society of the east coast states and carve out their fortunes in the expanding territories of the western frontier – where, incidentally, Smiles was a best-seller – the enthusiasm for Whitman's democratic vistas began to wear thin before the end of the nineteenth century. American industrialists discovered, like George Hudson in Britain, that competition was only profitable up to a certain point, and began to combine into monopolistic groupings, or 'trusts'. Less was then said about 'self-help' and competition, and more about 'the survival of the fittest', and American wealth, instead of helping to create a new culture of democracy, started buying up European works of art and marrying itself into the European aristocracy.

Now the attitude of people like Smiles and Whitman was well summed up by Matthew Arnold when he wrote:

> You think you have only to get on the back of your horse Freedom . . . and to ride away as hard as you can, to be sure of coming to the right destination.

The experience of this philosophy in practice was to bring people back to Arnold's position, and to demand that society plan to some extent the direction it expected to take, and use as the basis for this plan a conception of the full development of the individuals within it.

Let's look again in some detail at the two liberal thinkers, John Stuart Mill and Matthew Arnold, with the criticisms they made of unrestricted individualism. Essentially Mill and Arnold were liberals who believed that the break-up of traditional systems of authority had been beneficial to the individual, in that he had been left free to think for himself. However visually or even intellectually attractive past ages had been, society had then been divided into the privileged on one hand and the subservient on the other; it was parochial and prejudiced. (You will see this sort of liberal reaction to the not so distant past in George Eliot's description of the Midlands in *Industrialisation and Culture* B1). Industrialisation and political reform had necessarily broken this torpor, but the problem now was that individuals would grind themselves down

MILL'S LOGIC; OR, FRANCHISE FOR FEMALES.
"PRAY CLEAR THE WAY, THERE, FOR THESE—A—PERSONS."

Fig. 2 John Stuart Mill attempts to persuade Parliament to enfranchise women, 1867.

23

into a common and dull mediocrity, as competitive units in a situation in which the value of anything was determined by the supply of it and the demand for it in a mass market, and not by the talents and tastes of individuals themselves. Even faced with this, however, Mill and Arnold propounded remedies within the political structure of democratic government. Mill wanted government made more sensitive to minority interests through schemes of proportional representation and supported female suffrage, Arnold wanted the role of the state increased, especially in the field of education. Both, in a way, are fairly representative of the progress of liberal thought during the nineteenth century, from hostility to government action as an interference with individual liberty to approval of it as a safeguard of individual liberty. This ensured that the health of the slum-dweller was secured and that his children were adequately educated; without this intervention the liberty of such an individual was a fiction.

It is also possible to see the extension of the role of the state as a more directly defensive action on the part of the propertied classes. Some liberals had objections to popular government which were less metaphysical than those of Mill and Arnold. Robert Lowe, the tooth-and-nail opponent of the Reform Bill of 1866, pictured a working class ready to loot its betters as soon as it got a voice in parliament. This was no doubt an extreme position, and Lowe's predictions were defied by the facts, but even in the most optimistic Liberal writing of the period – James Bryce (*Industrialisation and Culture* H5) for instance – 'the ignorance and turbulence of that lowest class' makes the odd alarming appearance. Against ignorance and turbulence the remedy was also state action, to promote education, eliminate the worst slum areas where political discontent as well as disease were supposed to germinate, and in the last resort to preserve law and order. Lowe summed it up when he called for improved education after the passage of the 1867 Reform Act: 'I believe it will be absolutely necessary to compel our future masters to learn their letters'.

This 'interventionism' was no cut and dried programme but was built up gradually and in a piece-meal fashion, through parliamentary legislation, the role of government inspectors and officials, and the activities of local government.

EXERCISE

I want you to look through Part I of *Industrialisation and Culture* and see if you can detect two extracts which show this sort of intervention, then look over the correspondence material of Units 29 and 30 and see if you can detect another two. When you have located your extracts, enter them in the middle box below, putting in the left-hand box the reference number of the section or extract, and in the right-hand box note what or who you think was the *agent* of this intervention. There are three possibilities:

> parliamentary action
> government inspection
> local government action

G3	Ed. Chad.	Gov. insp.
G4	Educ. Bill	parl. action
3.5	Glasgow corp.	Local gov.
2.5	Rly. control	parl. action

SPECIMEN ANSWERS

G3	Edwin Chadwick's report on public health	government inspection
G4	W. E. Forster's speech on the 1870 Education Bill	parliamentary action
2.5	government control of railway rates	parliamentary action
3.5	municipal intervention in public health and transport	local government action

DISCUSSION

The point about all these examples of interventionism is that they are responses to situations *as they became critical*. Bad sanitation had to be tackled because it threatened the efficient operation of industry by reducing the productivity of labour, increased poverty by depriving families of their bread-winners, and menaced the health of everyone living in the great cities because of the way in which it assisted the spread of epidemic disease. Public education became a necessity because political reform made a literate electorate advisable, and foreign competition meant that Britain had to have a more skilled and adaptable labour force. The government had to fix railway rates in the public interest or face the prospect of railway companies combining to fix them in their own interests. Local government had to secure good water supply, adequate housing and cheap transport because a system geared to the profit motive was failing to cater for the needs of the mass of city dwellers.

Such interventions were 'pragmatic', in other words they were made in response to particular problems as they arose and not directly out of a view of the ideal relationships of man and society. But cumulatively they affected social philosophy. You will notice how in his sanitary report Edwin Chadwick couches his conclusions in language which he hopes will appeal to the devotees of an individualist economy who resent any measure of government interference. What he is saying is: 'You are not going to get your free economy working at all adequately if you permit its labour force to be attacked by disease. So, allow the government to intervene at this level, and it can create a situation in which free enterprise can work, and having done that, need do no more.'

EXERCISE

If you were a really doctrinaire believer in 'laissez-faire' what flaw would you see in this argument?

ANSWER IN MARGIN

SPECIMEN ANSWER

To the confirmed believer in 'laissez-faire' the unrestricted play of the laws of economics offered a solution to all social problems. For instance, if there was a sufficient demand for a supply of pure water, a commercial company would be attracted by the prospect of profit to provide a supply. If manufacturers found that siting their factories in cities meant that they lost working hours because of diseases which affected their employees, they could move their factories into country areas. If workers could not afford good housing, they should either press for higher wages, limit the size of their families, or migrate to where wages were higher. For government to intervene to solve a social problem, even if it gave the excuses that Chadwick gave, meant that the ability of 'market economics' to solve this problem was denied, and an 'unnatural' situation was maintained.

DISCUSSION

The point made here is really that the ideal state of the advocates of 'laissez-faire' was essentially a utopian one. It presupposed a flexibility in economic and social arrangements which did not exist. Even for manufacturers, who might formally be committed to economic individualism, the dislocation of moving factories out of cities, away from markets, was greater than that of bending the laws of economics to make city organisation more tolerable. And once one exception to the rule of 'laissez-faire' was made, others followed, in education, transport and the operation of public utilities.

All these might be done by men who would be appalled if their activities were described as socialistic, by Conservative and Liberal governments and by local councils and their officials. They might all be excused in the same terms as Chadwick, but gradually they had the effect of reducing the dominance of the ideology of 'laissez-faire'. By the 1880s, when the Liberty and Property Defence League was formed to resist what it termed 'the socialistic inclinations' of governments, both conservative and liberal, it merely collected a few rather antique aristocrats and semi-anarchist cranks. When the liberal chancellor of the exchequer, Sir William Harcourt, said in 1894 'We are all socialists now' he meant that the idea of public intervention had now been accepted as a fact of life.

So, by the end of our period, the idea of intervening to control the consequences of industrial progress had in fact been incorporated into the process of industrialisation itself.

With this came a change in the identity of the individual in industrial society, a move away from the anonymous 'economic man' towards a realisation that men in industrial society were human beings, with relationships and needs which ought to be respected and catered for by government.

SECTION 3

THE CONSCIOUSNESS OF THE WORKING CLASS

In section 2 we have been looking at the ideology of the ruling group in society. We have seen how it had to be remodelled to respond when challenged by forces created by the industrial growth that it was so closely associated with. We have seen something of the role of liberal thinkers like John Stuart Mill and Matthew Arnold in this process. But what we must not forget is that the number of people they addressed was tiny, even if it was influential.

One way of visualising the size and nature of this group is to look at the newspapers and periodicals that it read. Let us look first of all at three national newspapers of our own day, *The Times*, the *Daily Telegraph* and the *Guardian*. In 1860 the 'Top People' numbered about 65,000, the *Telegraph* reached about double that number. The population of England and Wales was then about 20,000,000. The *Manchester Guardian*, as it was then, was the organ of the industrial north-west; in 1842, when the population of Lancashire alone was 1,600,000, its circulation was 8,000. But the sort of social discussions in which Arnold and Mill took part were carried on less in newspapers than in monthly and quarterly reviews, which paid well for articles and provided employment for a fair number of professional men and academics. The radical *Fortnightly Review* (which in typical British fashion appeared monthly) to which both Arnold and Mill contributed, had a circulation of 2,500 in 1870. The biggest, the old established *Edinburgh Review*, reached about 15,000.

What this indicates is a tiny 'educated' minority – not much more than a quarter of a million at the most – a fact which gives reality to the fears of the liberals of the 1860s at being swamped by the mass. Here you seem to have a vivid example of the sort of social development in a capitalist state predicted by Karl Marx – on one side the men of business and the professional people associated with the apparatus of education, law and religion they supported, on the other the millions of wage-earners from whose labour their wealth was derived. It took about two days' labour for a ploughman to earn enough to buy a copy of the *Fortnightly Review* at 2/-, should he be so inclined, and in it he might discover an article on the miseries of the agricultural labourer for which an Oxford academic had been paid more than he could earn in a year.

However, the revolutionary political activity that Marx and his colleague Engels expected to result from such a polarisation (see Engels on trade unions in *Industrialisation and Culture* G1) did not in fact come about. In the 1870s, as you can see from the introduction to the extract, Engels was deploring the exclusively industrial preoccupations of British trade unionism. Later he welcomed the foundation of the Independent Labour Party in 1893 as evidence of a more militant spirit, but in 1914 he would have been disappointed to note that, whereas in France and Germany there were substantial socialist parties organised on 'scientific socialist' and theoretically revolutionary lines, the British Labour Party was neither scientific in its socialism, nor even mildly revolutionary.

In 1914 the Labour Party had 39 M.Ps, led by Keir Hardie,

who had been elected as the M.P. for West Ham, London, in 1892. This strength was achieved largely by an arrangement with the ruling Liberals (who had then 275 seats) which allowed Labour candidates, mainly trade unionists, a straight fight with Conservatives in certain working-class constituencies.

To this extent, therefore, the Labour Party was more or less the trade union wing of the Liberals. However, behind the M.Ps stood an energetic political movement, with magazines, debating groups, and clubs and societies of all descriptions, which had over the preceding twenty years taken a progressively greater role in the lives not only of working people, but of middle-class intellectuals from the same sort of background as Mill and Arnold. Yet the socialism to which they assented with almost religious fervour was derived less from the economic analysis of Marx and Engels, than from the rationalisation of a pattern of social relationships peculiar to Britain, reinforced by the writing of indigenous critics of industrial society.

In the radio broadcast associated with this unit Professor Iain Gregor mentions that when the thirty Labour M.Ps elected in 1906 were asked which book most influenced them, most of them replied: John Ruskin's *Unto this Last*. In the sections which follow we will be discussing in some detail the arguments, style and vocabulary of Ruskin and the critical tradition in which he stood. In the rest of this unit I want to look at the other side of the equation: what were the elements in the make-up of the developing Labour movement which made it receptive to the contribution of this tradition?

Before we start, however, a word about procedure. I thought it advisable to precede discussion of the social thought of Carlyle and Ruskin and their literary influence by placing them in their social and economic context. This creates problems: not the least being the obvious one that you have to know something about the thought of Carlyle and Ruskin before you can put it in context. My own feeling is that the changes in working-class culture were themselves so significant in influencing the thought of contemporary social commentators that they should be dealt with first. But, in order to get a rough idea of the dimensions of Carlyle and Ruskin's criticism, I would first read through sections 4 and 5 and then return to this section.

EXERCISE

We are going to look first at working-class life before industrialisation. I want you to try to recollect where in the course material (including the radio and television supplements) of Units 29–30 and *Industrialisation and Culture* there are three descriptions of cultural situations which seem to you to exemplify pre-industrial society. Specify them in the boxes below, and explain your choice.

> 1.

2.

3.

Now turn to the list of adjectives below: which would you select if you had to describe the sort of society these extracts describe? (Ring the appropriate ones.)

insular	utilitarian	traditional	customary
energetic	rational	intimate	paternal
innovatory	deferential	economic	self-contained
literate	instinctive	libertarian	organic

SPECIMEN ANSWERS

The three extracts I chose were:

> 1. The description of the villages around Swindon in the supplement to the radio programme *Life in a Railway Factory*, which noted their self-sufficiency, their traditional customs, but also their insularity.

> 2. George Eliot's description of Midland village life in *Felix Holt* (*Industrialisation and Culture* B1), rather similar to the above, but dwelling also on the illiteracy and credulity of the villagers.

> 3. The former close relationships between farmer and farm-hand William Cobbett remembered when watching the farm sale at Dorking (*Industrialisation and Culture* F1).

The adjectives which I felt described the sort of society indicated in them were:

insular   traditional   customary

intimate   paternal

deferential   self-contained

instinctive   organic

DISCUSSION

The society of the pre-industrial working class was essentially the close-knit one of the country village. The closest bonds were those of family and work relationships and local traditions. The folk-culture that these gave rise to was not literary but verbal and customary, embodied in stories, songs and traditions which had a close relevance to the need of the community for social cohesion: in other words, a culture that was closer in many respects to that of African or Asian village communities than to that of post-industrial Britain.

Now it's fairly easy to imagine what happened to such a structure of relationships when agriculture was reorganised on a commercial basis, a process which took place with increasing rapidity throughout the eighteenth century. The identity of culture and community life began to break up, and this process was accelerated by the rapid development of industry and the growth of the towns. A verbal, traditional culture depends on *continuity*. Even if we believe that the material benefits industrialisation brought outweighed the costs it exacted, it was a dramatic *discontinuity* in the lives of those who participated in it. The old culture was not totally destroyed – as we shall see, it, or the memory of it, continued to figure in a shadowy way in the politics of the new urban working class – but it ceased to play a vital role in relating urban workmen to their work or to each other. A new culture had to be created for an industrial working class.

In Units 29 and 30 we dwelt at some length on the process of industrialisation itself, and later on, at the beginning of this unit, we summed up the costs and benefits of the changes. You will re-member that at the end of Unit 30 we looked at the new sorts of commodities and experiences industrialisation made available to the inhabitants of the largely urban Britain which entered the twentieth century. We noted how far these were the direct product of technical improvements in production and distribution, how far they were made more readily available because of a more prosperous community, and how far legislation had to be invoked to make them generally accessible. By and large these improvements in life were made available either simply through the operation of commercial enterprise by itself, or by action on the part of bodies which, like central and local government, represented the whole of society.

EXERCISE

Now I want you to look at a description of a mature industrial community – Beatrice Webb's passage on Bacup (*Industrialisation and Culture* G5). What are the two agencies of improvement she noticed there? How do they differ from the sort of action described above?

31

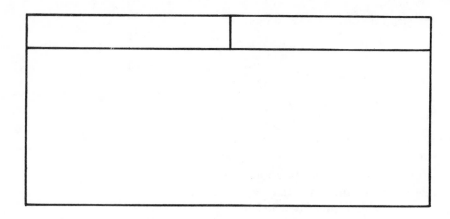

SPECIMEN ANSWER

co-operative stores	working class nonconformity
The common factor in both is that they are organised from within the working class as a response to the situation created by industrial change.	

DISCUSSION

Co-operation, like trade unionism, was a response which came from within the working class. Although there were numerous precedents, the modern movement really dates from 1844, when the Rochdale Society of Equitable Pioneers established what became the organisational prototype of co-ops throughout the country. The Co-operative Wholesale Society was founded in 1863, and the Co-operative Union in 1869, a year after the first meeting of its trade union equivalent, the Trades Union Congress. Although both institutions accepted capitalist industrial society, and proclaimed that they existed to humanise it rather than to destroy it, they were the creation of working people and components of their new self-awareness as a class.

We can see the same sort of ambiguity in working-class religion. At the same time as the first major wave of industrialisation, between about 1770 and 1830, there was a revolution in religious belief in Britain, begun by the missionary activity of the Wesleys and broadened by what we call the Evangelical Revival. By concentrating on inculcating puritan standards of individual conduct in rich and poor alike, and enforcing these by reference to a literal interpretation of scripture, the vocabulary and imagery of religion were deeply implanted in the developing society of the industrial working class.

EXERCISE

Now I want you to look at two other passages by mid-nineteenth-century writers which describe the effect such 'vital religion' had on the working-class community. The first is from John Morley, the editor of the radical *Fortnightly Review*, for the second see the passage from George Eliot's *Felix Holt* in *Industrialisation and Culture* B1, p.33. Then I want you to enter in the boxes below:

1. What function did evangelical religion perform for industrial society?

2. What sentence in George Eliot suggests that it did not simply perform this function and leave it at that?

Here is the passage from Morley:

> Although the theology of a town like Blackburn is of a narrow, rancorous kind, yet one must give even this dull and cramped Evangelicalism its due, and admit that the churches and chapels have done a good service through their Sunday Schools and otherwise in impressing a kind of moral organisation on the mass of barbarism which surged chaotically into the factory towns. Lancashire theology does not make a man love his neighbour; but its external system promotes cleanliness, truth-telling and chastity; and the zeal of the clergy of all sects, however much we may wish that it had been connected with a more hopeful doctrine, has been a barrier, for which civilisation will always owe something to their name, against the most awful influx the world ever saw of furious provocatives to unbridled sensuality and riotous animalism.

1.

2.

SPECIMEN ANSWERS

1. Evangelical religion, through its discipline and its educational activities, conditioned a displaced population to the new and unfamiliar experience of urban and industrial life.

2. The passage:

> Here was a population not convinced that the old England was as good as possible; here were multitudinous men and women aware that their religion was not exactly the religion of their rulers, who might therefore be better than they were, and who, if better, might alter many things which now made the world perhaps more painful than it need be, and certainly more sinful.

indicates that Nonconformist religion became a vehicle for social protest.

DISCUSSION

Although evangelical religion could be, and was used, as the 'opiate of the people', to stifle social discontents, it penetrated so deeply into the consciousness of the new working-class communities that it profoundly affected working-class culture and politics. Non-conformity, with its traditions going back to the puritan and republican seventeenth century, was quite alien to the Established Church to which the leaders of the Whig and Tory parties, the public schools and the universities – in a word, the *Establishment*, belonged. It provided the bond which, until the First World War, held the heterogenous components of the Liberal party and its allies – provincial businessmen, labour and small farmers – together.

As Beatrice Webb noticed, non-conformity also gave the working-class experience, through the self-governing chapels, in independent organisation. But probably most important, it gave it the forceful imagery and vocabulary of the pulpit. Here is the farm labourer's leader, Joseph Arch, describing a recruiting campaign in the 1870s:

> There was anger and amazement among the powers of the land – the lord, the squire, the farmer, the parson – when they saw these serfs of the soil girding on their manhood, and heard them refuse to starve any longer on nine and ten shillings a week. Toilers in the north and in the south, in the west and in the east, stood still to watch and listen. Here were the lowest of their brethren, those who had been dumb with fear and stricken to the earth with want, holding themselves like men, and bracing themselves together for battle with the powers of darkness seated in high places. Their voice was gone abroad with no uncertain sound, and the noise of their moving was heard afar off. The grand day of their awakening had fully come.

EXERCISE

Here is a passage from another piece of political writing. In the margin, I want you to say which of the two appeals most *directly* to you, and why?

> The immediate task that confronts the class-conscious vanguard of the international labour movement is to be able to *lead* the broad masses (now, for the most part, slumbering, apathetic, hidebound, inert and dormant) to their new position, or, rather, to be able to lead *not only* their own Party and also the masses during the course of their approach, their transition to the new position. While the first historical task (vis., that of winning over the class-conscious vanguard of the proletariat to the side of the Soviet power and the dictatorship of the working class) could not be accomplished without a complete ideological and political victory over opportunism and social-chauvinism, the second task, which now becomes the immediate task, and which is to lead the *masses* to the new position that will assure the victory of the vanguard in the revolution, this immediate task cannot be accomplished without the liquidation of Left doctrinairism, without completely overcoming and getting rid of its mistakes.

ANSWER IN MARGIN

SPECIMEN ANSWER

My first inclination would be to prefer Arch's passage as it enlists our sympathy, albeit a bit long-windedly, for an obviously downtrodden group, and uses metaphors with which we are all familiar – 'powers of darkness' and so on. The second extract sounds abstract and scientific, and riddled with the cold terms we have come to associate with Communism – 'class-conscious vanguard', 'liquidation of Left doctrinairism'.

DISCUSSION

The second quotation is in fact from Lenin's *Left-Wing Communism: An Infantile Disorder*. Now it's possible you may respond to his language in a positive way, but I imagine the first thing you thought was 'communist cliché'. In fact the passage could be re-written in such a way that, without losing Lenin's meaning, you wouldn't have this reaction, but, in fact you would have a very long passage, as Lenin uses terms like 'class-conscious vanguard' as a shorthand for factors which it would take volumes to define, in the formulation of 'scientific socialism'. He is concerned to put over a clear strategy, in scientific terms, to a group of men similarly motivated and sharing the same grounding in Marxist socialist thought. This reflects the way the communists were organised, power resting with a small group of highly-educated, dedicated and intellectually convinced men. Lenin isn't concerned to convert the masses but to convince his colleagues.

Arch, on the other hand, is concerned to convert. The language he uses is Biblical, and it is directed to making the reader respond emotionally to it in the same emotional way that he would to a vehement sermon. And, although the language sounds overblown, it would not be totally out of place in a political speech today, even one delivered, say, by a Communist trade unionist. Apart from the language, the content is significant. The passage is a plea for sympathy, which presupposes that people who have no direct interest in helping the farmhands will nevertheless do so. As in fact they did; Arch got help from Liberal politicians, non-conformist ministers and middle-class radicals. The 'pulpit style' has in fact two functions in the passage: it states a class interest in the language of religious morality which the Warwickshire ploughman will recognise instantly, and it reaches out to appeal to the other social classes who share the institutions and antipathies of non-conformity.

Common to the three institutions we have been discussing – trade unionism, co-operation and non-conformity – was a quality unique to the British social situation. *Each institution contributed to the class-consciousness of the industrial work-force, but it also coexisted with the existing capitalist order.* This did not stop them pressing for reforms, and these reforms, when they came, both made the system less capitalist, as we have seen, and strengthened the position of the working-class institutions further in their turn. Liberal politicians who were apprehensive about what they thought might be a working-class state within the state were worried about the steady growth of the power of working-class institutions yet, ultimately, they had too much in common with the working class to move against it.

As we have seen, neither trade unionism, co-operation nor non-conformity were in themselves hostile to the capitalist industrial state, even when incorporated into working-class life. All three, for example, continued to coexist with capitalism in America. Yet the political ideology of the Labour movement in Britain was, by the turn of the century, definitely anti-capitalist. Here is a motion moved by Keir Hardie in the House of Commons in April 1901:

> That considering the increasing burden which the private ownership of land and capital is imposing on the industrious and useful classes of the community, the poverty and destitution and general moral and physical deterioration resulting from a competitive system of wealth production, the alarming growth of trusts and syndicates, able by reason of their great wealth to influence governments and plunge peaceful nations into war to serve their own interests, this House is of the opinion that such a state of matters is a menace to the well-being of the Realm and calls for legislation designed to remedy the same by inaugurating a Socialist Commonwealth founded upon the common ownership of land and capital, production for use and not for profit, and equality of opportunity for every citizen.

The motion was, of course, defeated, but it expressed the mind of the younger generation who were taking control of the institutions of the working class, the generation Beatrice Webb, herself shortly to join them, had seen moving from the chapels to politics. Now there were several reasons for this more resolute formulation of socialist goals, most of which we have already looked at:

1. The extension of the powers of the state and of working-class organisations could create a philosophy of the gradual supplanting of community or 'collectivist' control for competitive enterprise.

2. Economic recession during the eighties and nineties meant, as we saw in section 3 of our study of Glasgow, a confrontation of capital and labour and extensive industrial unrest.

3. The influence of explicitly anti-capitalist ideologies.

Now there is nothing explicitly socialist about 1. You could have powerful working-class institutions without a socialist programme, as in America, or state intervention without a socialist programme, as in Germany. And, in the case of 2, there had been recessions before the eighties, and the response of the working class to them had not been a socialist one. Ideological change seems to be the new and critical factor. But what ideology?

Not Marxism, certainly. We have seen earlier that British socialism was not revolutionary. A minority did accept the Marxist analysis of the need for revolutionary struggle, including William Morris, but like him most of them reached Marx after stating their objection to capitalism in moral terms rather than analysing its likely development (see *Industrialisation and Culture* H 12). The ideology was emphatically one of moral dissent from capitalism, directed at the imagination and moral sensibilities of a working class which was now, thanks to the Board Schools, literate, and preached by literary men of the middle class. And the core of their arguments lay in the tradition of social criticism essentially begun by Carlyle and reinforced by Ruskin, which we shall examine in detail in the next section. Even if they quoted them only to disagree with them, Bernard Shaw, H. G. Wells, Oscar Wilde, Robert Blatchford, Edward Carpenter and other disturbers of the late Victorian peace took their texts from Carlyle and Ruskin.

Before we end this section, one problem, surely, remains to be cleared up. What causes a middle-class intellectual to express grave doubts about the future of capitalist society, since he himself is pre-eminently a product of it? And why should such profound criticisms of the industrial order be transmitted from them to the working class, instead of the other way about?

EXERCISE

I want you to read through the extract from *The Deliverance of Mark Rutherford* in *Industrialisation and Culture* P8.

1. How would you describe the pattern of life associated with this job?

2. Can you think of a present-day job which draws similar comments?

3. Whose reaction do you think would be strongest to the demands imposed by this job – a manual labourer or a middle-class literary man? And why?

SPECIMEN ANSWERS

1.

The pattern of life associated with this job is the monotonous repetition of a single simple task.

2.

The sort of present-day job that this seems to resemble most is one where a worker continually fits nuts to bolts on an assembly-line.

3.

The strongest reaction would, I think, come from the literary man, as he has a higher expectation of the mental satisfaction offered by work which involves initiative and imagination. A manual labourer, probably doing boring and repetitive work for a low wage, would prefer work which was even more boring and repetitive if the increase in wages was sufficiently high to compensate for it.

DISCUSSION

For the workers in a developing industrial society the immediate interest at stake was the survival of themselves and their families. Unpleasant conditions and monotonous routine in the factory were preferable to near-starvation on the land or at the hand-loom. Alfred Williams noticed this at Swindon; few of his workmates did – they never questioned what they considered a patent improvement. Middle-class commentators were much more apprehensive about the long-term consequences of such a regime. We have seen already in the case of Arnold and Mill their apprehension at the prospect of a growing human uniformity and at the possible effect of the mass-democracy on individual and cultural values. If we add to this disquiet the perception that through the excessive specialisation of his work and the continuous discipline of industrial life the worker is coming more and more to resemble a machine, the position of the middle-class commentator becomes thoroughly hostile to the pre-vailing system. The industrial working class ceases to be simply another political interest but something which could become, if the system of exploitation and mechanisation was continued, something totally alien, either kept to its machines by ruthless force or imposing its dehumanised rule on the rest of society. In H. G. Wells' fantasy *The Time Machine* (1895) the time traveller alights in a future London to find the flower-children members of a former ruling class – the Eloi – kept for food by the Morlocks, who live in great factory-tunnels underground. He rationalises the situation:

> . . . it seemed clear as daylight to me that the gradual widening of the present merely temporary and social difference between the Capitalist and the Labourer, was the key to the whole position. No doubt it will seem grotesque enough to you – and wildly incredible! – and yet even now there are existing circumstances to point that way. There is a tendency to utilize underground space for the less ornamental purposes of civilization. . . . Even now, does not an East-end worker live in such artificial conditions as practically to be cut off from the natural surface of the earth?

38

Now this is from a sensational work of science fiction, not social criticism, and the position stated is an extreme development. Yet it is an extreme development of tendencies which were recognised to be present in Victorian society. 'Men are grown mechanical in head and heart', wrote Carlyle in *Signs of the Times*. 'You must either make a tool of the creature, or a man of him', wrote Ruskin. In *Industrialisation and Culture* you also have Mark Rutherford's pathetic clerk and, later on, D. H. Lawrence's description of the holidaying Londoner marching over the Alps like a clockwork toy. (*Industrialisation and Culture* A1, M3, P8, P15.) All testify to the dehumanising effect of industrial society, the mechanisation of relationships, and indicate the possibility of the extinction both of individual integrity and traditional culture. This perception was not the only one articulated by intellectuals which was then incorporated into the ideology of working-class politics, but it was, I think, the critical one, through which the intellectuals came to realise that their predicament and that of the industrial workers were inextricably linked.

THE BRITISH SOCIAL CRITICS

We have been looking at how the social philosophy of industrial society changed from belief in a free for all to belief in a degree of conscious planning and intervention on the part of public bodies. Then we studied the institutions of the working class and saw where the contribution of Victorian social critics was relevant in the evolution of its politics. Now we are going to study these critics in detail, their arguments and the language in which they expressed them.

We have already seen that the tradition of social criticism formulated by British men of letters was quite distinct from the 'scientific socialism' which by the end of the century had been accepted by working-class political parties in most of the nations of Europe. Two important elements clearly differentiate this British tradition from its European counterpart. These are: the presence in the British critics of a strong religious element; and the nature of their techniques of style and language, which are essentially *creative*.

The critics in this section are all creative writers: some are novelists, some poets; others, like Carlyle and Ruskin, used creative techniques to speak directly about social conditions. This means simply that they tried to dramatise and make concrete their statements; to express their meanings through imagery and the 'poetic' organisation of language; to communicate their experience, and make it present to the reader, as well as commenting on it in a more abstract way.

The use of creative language enables the writer to make his statements more vividly, in a more impressive and exciting way; but it involves more than mere rhetorical emphasis. Techniques of creative language can make social criticism in itself – without reference to its practical effectiveness – more complex, more effective and more valuable than abstract 'scientific' criticism. So in this part of the unit we'll be undertaking some close analysis of language and style, in order to evaluate the social critics' use of creative language.

The religious element is more difficult. We ought at this point to attempt a definition of the word 'religious' as it's used in the following pages. Perhaps *definition* is the wrong word, it implies a sense of fixed and absolute certainty about meaning which is inappropriate to a complex word (and one that radically changes its meaning during the period under discussion). Let's start with two dictionary definitions, both from the *Oxford English Dictionary*.

RELIGION

1. A particular system of faith or worship.

2. Recognition on the part of man of some higher unseen power as having control over his destiny, and as being entitled to obedience, reverence and worship; the general mental and moral attitude resulting from such a belief, with reference to its effects upon the individual or the community; personal or general acceptance of this feeling as a standard.

Most of the social critics we will be dealing with were brought up as Christians, either within the Established Church or the non-conformist sects – within, in other words, a 'particular system of faith or worship'. That's our first definition. Religion in this sense is a clearly defined theological and moral orthodoxy, an accepted form of ritual and worship, and a conception of the nature of God.

Responding to a widespread movement of rationalist criticism of religion, which owed its growing effectiveness partly to advances in the natural sciences, partly to the slackening of the social pressures which had sustained evangelical religion as a means of social control, all these social critics found the acceptance of a 'particular system of faith and worship' impossible. But, even when scientific criticism destroyed religious belief, 'the general mental and moral attitude resulting from such a belief' (our second definition) remained. So religion remains an important source of ideas and convictions in the social critics, although the basic religious belief had radically changed, or disappeared altogether.

Read again the passage from Whitman's *Democratic Vistas* on p. 19. Note down the words, phrases or sentences which are properly religious vocabulary (leaving out the word *religion* itself).

ANSWER IN MARGIN

SPECIMEN ANSWER

Here are some possible answers:

'It has few full *believers* . . . it is not yet the *absolute faith* . . . has begotten them in spirit and in form . . . *monastics and ascetics* . . . *a new earth and a new man*.'

DISCUSSION

Whitman is talking about democracy, but he is using the traditional language and concepts of religion. Democracy can be seen as an 'absolute faith' commanding the allegiance of 'full believers' and dedicated 'monastics and ascetics'. Like all religions, it is the expression of a deep-rooted moral conviction in men, and like Catholic or Nonconformist Christianity will eventually bring about an apocalyptic milennium, a 'new heaven and a new earth'. The interesting thing about Whitman's interpretation of religion is that he is able to combine a traditional religious conviction (which is really just *belief* in something as an absolute truth) with a belief in the determinism common to relatively new modes of thought. Thus, democracy is a spontaneous and irreversible development, like Darwin's theory of evolution, like Marx's superseding of bourgeoisie by proletariat.

More than any other thinker, Thomas Carlyle contributed to this process of secularisation whereby, under the impact of scientific ideas, Christianity was interpreted into a secular basis. It was mainly through Carlyle that certain beliefs – in a quality of the divine in human nature, a religious element existing apart from organised social religion, and in a morality unsupported by orthodox Christian faith – were transmitted to many nineteenth-century intellectuals in the form of a moral, non-spiritual, secular religion. The historian J. A. Froude described how Carlyle's books, while showing him that the religion of his upbringing was an outworn symbol, enforced upon him the 'overpowering obligation' of duty, of moral responsibility; and George Eliot, who was deeply influenced by Carlyle, once told a friend how inconceivable she found the idea of God, how unbelievable the concept of immortality, but how peremptory and absolute the demands of Duty. Through Carlyle religion became secularised and rendered concrete, humanised and diverted in the direction of moral and social action.

So Christianity remains an important element in the English tradition of social criticism; an important source for the ideas and relationships which the social critics used in their analysis of the machine – symbol of all the social, economic and political changes that were transforming society. But when you find the word *religion* in the following pages, it means something different from orthodox Christianity. Each writer has his own particular interpretation; so the examination of each critic will demand a slightly different definition of 'religious'. Nonetheless, the religious element is the principal distinction between English social criticism and the scientific criticism of the European thinkers.

CARLYLE AND SECULAR RELIGION

You have read Carlyle's account of the Irish labourers (*Industrialisation and Culture* H8). The passage below also comes from *Chartism*, shortly before the extract in the anthology. It is placed here for comparison with a passage on the same subject from Friedrich Engels. Read the two descriptions, then answer the question.

> The rapid extension of English industry could not have taken place if England had not possessed in the numerous and impoverished population of Ireland a reserve at command. The Irish had nothing to lose at home, and much to gain in England: and from the time it became known in Ireland that the east side of St. George's Channel offered steady work and good pay for strong arms, every year has brought armies of the Irish hither. It has been calculated that more than a million have already immigrated, and not far from fifty thousand still come every year, nearly all of whom enter the industrial districts, especially the great cities, and there form the lowest class of the population. Thus there are in London, 120,000; in Manchester, 40,000; in Liverpool, 34,000; Bristol, 24,000; Glasgow, 40,000; Edinburgh, 29,000, poor Irish people. These people having grown up almost without civilization, accustomed from youth to every sort of privation, rough, intemperate, and improvident, bring all their brutal habits with them among a class of the English population which has, in truth, little inducement to cultivate education and morality.
>
> (*Engels*)

> The Sanspotato is of the selfsame stuff as the superfinest Lord Lieutenant. Not an individual sanspotato human scarecrow but had a life given him out of Heaven, with Eternities depending on it;

Fig. 3 Famine in Ireland – the alternative to the slums.

THE FAMINE IN IRELAND.—FUNERAL AT SKIBBEREEN.—FROM A SKETCH BY MR. H. SMITH, CORK.—(SEE NEXT PAGE.)

for once and no second time. With Immensities in him, over him and around him; with feelings which a Shakespeare's speech would not utter; with desires as illimitable as the Autocrat's of all the Russias.

(Carlyle)

Let's look closely at the Carlyle passage first. It's a concentrated and difficult piece, so read it again carefully. Carlyle begins by saying that each Irish pauper (sanspotato) is not essentially different in *quality* from the wealthy and powerful statesman (the Lord Lieutenant of Ireland); even though their material circumstances differ so widely. Two main points are made about the nature of this quality, which relates all human beings together. Say what they are in your own words.

ANSWER IN MARGIN

SPECIMEN ANSWERS

1. The quality is a religious one – every single individual nature embodies an element of the divine.
2. This divine element gives every individual an intrinsic greatness, or potential greatness, which is independent of external and material circumstances.

Now look again at the Engels passage. What is the main difference between the two writers in their attitude to the labourers?

ANSWER IN MARGIN

SPECIMEN ANSWER

Engels in this passage speaks of people as statistics – a series of numbers – and as classes or groups within a larger unit, the population. Carlyle focusses on each single person as an individual.

DISCUSSION

So while Engels sees society as a mass of units with certain material problems in common, Carlyle tries to see and understand each individual as a knowable person, to establish an identity of relationship, a community of feeling.

Carlyle essentially differs from Engels in rejecting completely the ideas of equality that were the legacy of the eighteenth-century enlightenment. This equality, realised in the idea of men as separate economic units, was common to the capitalist defenders of industrialisation and European thinkers like Marx and Engels whose sympathies lay not with the industrial innovator but with the men he exploited. Marxism was in a way simply the classical laws of economics followed out to a conclusion in which they destroyed themselves. These laws, Marx and Engels saw, did not promote in practice an equalisation of property. Instead they produced an imbalance of wealth. It followed, they argued, that this was in fact their real tendency, and that it was also their tendency to produce a labouring class swelling in size and dwindling in wealth, which

44

oner or later would successfully divest its exploiters of their wealth.

Carlyle is looking at society from a religious point of view, believing that the spiritual element in human nature is of absolute importance. From this religious concept of individuality Carlyle derived a sense of the *importance* of the individual, which is a strong element in his social criticism. The developments in industrial society which appeared to threaten the individual, were to Carlyle blasphemies – abuses of the element of God in man. The weakness of this position is that, unlike the socialism of Engels, it's a moral rather than a practical belief. It was very easy to interpret such a sense of the importance of spiritual things into an excuse for leaving material things exactly as they were. In the later Carlyle, something like this actually happened.

But let's look more closely for a moment at what happened to Carlyle's religious belief itself.

Carlyle was the son of a Scottish stonemason, and brought up as a Calvinist. He attended Edinburgh University to study for a ministry in the Church. There his Calvinistic puritanism was subjected to the kind of criticism referred to above; and it emerged no longer a fully dogmatic and rationalised religious faith, but a highly personal structure of emotional convictions and moral certainties. The mature Carlyle retained an unshaken faith in an omnipresent God, and in a living universe expressing a self-evident divine reality: in this he was an 'upholder of the spiritual view of the universe in an age of increasing materialism and unbelief'. But this faith was accompanied by a dissatisfaction with the established forms of religion, and a belief that Church and State were outworn symbols requiring regeneration. He abandoned his intention of a career within the Church.

Carlyle's prose derives much of its power from its adaptation of the language of the Authorised Version. Look at the quotations listed below. Two are from the Bible; two from Carlyle. Can you see which is which?

A.   'The strong have eated sour grapes, and the teeth of the weak are set on edge.'

B.   'The earth is good, and bountifully sends (forth) food and increase.'

C.   'The earth is full of the goodness of the Lord . . . for the earth bringeth forth fruit of herself . . . the earth shall yield her increase.'

D.   'The fathers have eaten sour grapes, and the teeth of the children are set on edge.'

ANSWER IN MARGIN

SPECIMEN ANSWER

> In fact the first two (A and B) are from 'Chartism'; C and D from the Old and New Testaments. But I think you'd agree that, without prior knowledge of the quotations, it would be natural to assume that they were all from the Bible.

(The Biblical passages are: C: Psalms 33, 5; Mark 4, 28; Ezekiel 34, 27. D is Ezekiel 18, 2)

Look now at these two statements, which are characteristic of Carlyle's philosophy of life. What is he doing with his religious material?

'*History:* the only epic poem and Universal *Divine Scripture*.'

'*Work* is *Worship*.'

ANSWER IN MARGIN

SPECIMEN ANSWER

> Carlyle is secularising the basic elements of religious belief. He substitutes secular history for sacred; and practical work for prayer or ritual worship.

DISCUSSION

In the same way he replaces the Bible with Literature, and a personal God with a divine but formless Infinite. The logical development of this process of translation is the belief that the divine expresses itself through concrete reality, and is evident in concrete experience:

> Through every star, through every blade of grass, is not a God made visible, if we will open our minds and eyes? . . . we recognise how every object has a divine beauty in it; how every object still verily is 'a window through which we may look into infinitude itself'.

And the most complex and highly developed expression of God is the human:

> We are the miracle of miracles, the great inscrutable mystery of God.

You have seen how profound the relationship is between Carlyle's language and that of the Bible; and also how unorthodox his ideas are, how radically critical of formal Christianity. So in Carlyle's the language of the Bible is being put to a secular purpose; and this is an example of the way in which the nineteenth-century social critics applied the vocabulary, the ideas, the traditional wisdom of Christianity to modern social conditions; as Carlyle uses the words of Ezekiel to speak about the Irish labourers.

Now look at this passage from Carlyle's book, *Heroes and Hero Worship*. This book continues the process of secularisation by translating the saints or holy men of religion into Heroes, who can be pagan prophets, poets, political leaders or men of letters.

> We cannot look, however imperfectly, on a great man, without gaining something by him. He is the living light-fountain, which it is good and pleasant to be near. The light which enlightens, which has enlightened the darkness of the world; and this not as a kindled lamp only, but rather as a natural luminary shining out of Heaven.

You probably noticed that Carlyle uses a Biblical echo here, recalling the famous words of Christ: 'I am the light of the world: he that followeth me shall not walk in darkness, but shall have the light of life.' (John 8, 12.) What is the significance of that Biblical echo?

ANSWER IN MARGIN

SPECIMEN ANSWER

> Carlyle is transferring the responsibility which in the Gospel belongs to Christ – the responsibility for lightening the moral darkness of the world – to human beings. Once again, it's a characteristic aspect of his secularisation.

DISCUSSION

So the work which, in orthodox Christianity is left to Christ, in Carlyle's religion has to be done by men – who are themselves almost Godlike – 'natural luminaries shining *out* of heaven'. The responsibility for social amelioration is placed on individual action and moral regeneration, rather than on the political reorganisation of society envisaged by Marx and Engels. Carlyle's religion is really Christianity without Christ.

This is how the religious sense of individuality distinguishes Carlyle from the European thinkers, Marx and Engels. They saw society being changed by impersonal forces and movements: the accumulation of wealth according to the laws of economics; the struggle for political power between social groups, class-warfare. In Carlyle the condition of society is a direct consequence of the actions of individuals; and the moral regeneration of those individuals could bring about changes for the better in society itself.

The Carlyle who wrote the above statement simply wouldn't have accepted Marx's famous statement in the *Critique of Political Economy*, that:

> The mode of production in material life determines the general character of the social, political and spiritual processes of life. It is not the consciousness of men that determines their existence, but on the contrary, their social existence determines their consciousness.

And yet Carlyle's earliest social criticism reveals a clear perception of the relation between 'the mode of production' and 'the general character of the social, political and spiritual processes of life'. In fact, 'Signs of the Times' could have provided Marx and Engels with a starting-point. Let's look now at this great statement of Carlyle's response to the machine.

SECTION 6

CREATIVITY AND INDUSTRIALISM

Read the extract from *Signs of the Times* in *Industrialisation and Culture* A1. In this passage, Carlyle uses the words 'machinery' and 'mechanical' in two different ways; and the two senses constitute the basic structure of his argument.

1. Can you see what the two meanings are? Copy out in the lower boxes the sentences representing each meaning.

```
The first sense in which machinery is used is:



```

```
The second sense is:



```

2. When Carlyle says 'men have grown *mechanical* in head and heart' in which sense is the word used?

```



```

1. The first sense in which 'machinery' is used is:
the machine as a physical object.

'On every hand, the living artisan is driven from his workshop, to make room for a speedier, inanimate one. The shuttle drops from the fingers of the weaver, and falls into iron fingers that ply it faster. The sailor furls his sail, and lays down his oar; and bids a strong, unwearied servant, on vaporous wings, bear him through the waters. Men have crossed oceans by steam; the Birmingham Fire-king has visited the fabulous East; and the genius of the Cape, were there any Camoens now to sing it, has again been alarmed, and with far stranger thunders than Gamas. There is no end to machinery.'

The second sense is:
comprehensive 'mechanisation' of life.

'Not the external and physical alone is now managed by machinery, but the internal and spiritual also. . . . Has any man, or any society of men, a truth to speak, a piece of spiritual work to do; they can nowise proceed at once with the mere natural organs, but must first call a public meeting, appoint committees, issue prospectuses, eat a public dinner; in a word, construct or borrow machinery, wherewith to speak it and do it.'

2. He refers not to the machines themselves, but to certain changes in human nature – so the word is used in its metaphorical sense.

DISCUSSION

The argument of this passage is not simple: so to isolate the main points, we'll have to break it down.

Carlyle begins by referring to the machines themselves (para. 1). He then goes on to describe (para. 2) material changes – changes in the physical standard of living (mostly for the better), changes in the structure of society (for the worse) – which accompany the widespread use of machinery. In the third, fourth and fifth paragraphs the argument becomes more complex, and we can see the words being transferred to their metaphorical senses: certain kinds of activity (classified as 'spiritual work') begin to take on a character unnatural to them by using 'mechanical' methods of organisation: education, which should be carefully gauged to individual needs and aptitudes, is conducted in a uniformly similar fashion; religion, by making use of the 'machinery' of advertising, publicity and subscription, closely involves itself with the ethics of capitalist society. Now this process, by which 'spiritual work' is executed by 'mechanical' modes of operation, brings about the most important change, the 'mechanisation' of the mind. This is expressed in the last paragraph.

So the transference of meaning from object to metaphor sums up the basic argument: that the influence of machinery causes an impersonal, *mechanical* quality to become an essential part of life.

Now look carefully at the *third* paragraph (p. 22). What main point is the metaphor making? Answer in one sentence.

Now look at the *final* paragraph, which sentence makes the main point here?

SPECIMEN ANSWERS

The 'mechanical' quality, by encroaching on the most important branches of cultural activity – Religion, Education, Philosophy, Science, Art, Literature – becomes a characteristic of all intellectual activity.

'Men have grown mechanical in head and heart' – These developments have profound implications for the way in which men think and feel about their relationship with each other, and with society.

DISCUSSION

For example, Carlyle thought that in an industrial system, where the relations between the working classes and their middle-class employers are confined to the commercial exchange of labour for wages, no bond of feeling, emotional sympathy, mutual loyalty or respect could exist: industrial society is held together by nothing which touches human values or feelings, but by what Carlyle called the merely *mechanical* bond of the 'cash-nexus'. Social disorder was an inevitable consequence of such a social organisation: and in his great work *Past and Present* (1843) Carlyle analysed the causes of this disorder; and described, through the idealised image of a mediaeval monastery, a hypothetical kind of society which is held together by bonds of human feeling and a sense of human responsibility and controlled by a pervading religious consciousness.

Here Carlyle was both drawing on and reinforcing a tradition of retrospection in social criticism. You have it in William Cobbett's passage on the farm sale at Dorking – the backward look at a past golden age of rural security and co-operation – but in general the Middle Ages were found to be a safer period to commemorate than the recent past, about which memories might differ. You can see, in A. W. N. Pugin's *Contrasted Towns* (1836), (*Industrialisation and Culture* H10) how the dislocation and destruction of modern industrialism – the ruined churches, the prominence of prison, poorhouse and toll-gate – is compared with what the devout artist imagined to be the co-operative and compassionate society of the mediaeval town.

Now read this passage from Charles Dickens' *Hard Times* (1854), which focusses on the individual living and working in an industrial system. What similarity to Carlyle do you notice in Dickens' view of human nature?

> Stephen bent over his loom, quiet, watchful, and steady. A special contrast, as every man was in the forest of looms where Stephen worked, to the crashing, smashing, tearing piece of mechanism at which he laboured. Never fear, good people of an anxious turn of mind, that Art will consign Nature to oblivion. Set anywhere, side by side, the work of GOD and the work of man; and the former, even though it be a troop of Hands of very small account, will gain in dignity from the comparison.
>
> So many hundred hands in this mill; so many hundred horse steam Power. It is known, to the force of a single pound weight, what the engine will do; but not all the calculators of the National Debt can tell me the capacity for good or evil, for love or hatred, for the decomposition of virtue into vice, or the reverse, at any single moment in the soul of one of these its quiet servants, with the composed faces and the regulated actions. There is no mystery in it: there is an unfathomable mystery in the meanest of them, for ever.
>
> Supposing we were to reverse our arithmetic for material objects, and to govern these awful unknown quantities by other means!

SPECIMEN ANSWER

> Dickens and Carlyle share a concept of *individual* human nature, which is articulated in religious terms. As Carlyle could see divinity in an Irish 'sanspotato', so Dickens can see an 'unfathomable mystery' in the meanest of the mill-hands.

DISCUSSION

In this passage Dickens makes an explicit contrast between the individual who is the work of God, and the machine which is the work of man. He then goes on to make a connection, as Carlyle had done, between scientific economy and the machines; contrasting both with human nature as perceived in a religious way. Political economy is incapable of understanding men as individuals: for such an understanding, we must go to the traditional wisdom embodied in religion.

The relationship between Dickens and Carlyle is a very close one, and very detailed. Look at this comparison of passages from the two writers.

> What wonderful accessions have thus been made, and are still making, to the *physical* power of mankind; how much better fed, clothed, lodged, and, in all *outward* respects, accommodated men now are, or might be, by a given quantity of labour, is a grateful reflection which forces itself on every one. What changes, too, this addition of power is introducing into the social system; how wealth has more and more increased, and at the same time gathered itself more into masses, increasing the distance between rich and poor.
>
> *(Carlyle)*

> These attributes of Coketown were in the main inseparable from the work by which it was sustained; against them were to be set off, comforts of life which found their way all over the world, and elegancies of life which made, we will not ask how much of the fine lady, who could scarcely bear to hear the place mentioned.
>
> *(Dickens)*

These passages say much the same thing. Summarise in the margin what is said.

SPECIMEN ANSWER

> Both writers are saying that while productive machinery materially enriches the quality of life, the material benefits are not evenly distributed over the whole of society. In fact, the material goods produced in a Lancashire textile mill, and the material profits acquired by industrial enterprise, were almost exclusively for the benefit of a much smaller social group than that of the workers whose labour supported the system.

The quotation from Dickens comes from *Industrialisation and Culture*, p. 380. It points a fairly simple intellectual relation between Dickens and Carlyle. If you look now at Dickens's fourth paragraph, and compare it with the third paragraph of *Signs of the Times* (*Industrialisation and Culture* A1) you'll see that Dickens takes over Carlyle's more complex statements as well. Can you see the main connection?

ANSWER IN MARGIN

SPECIMEN ANSWER

> Dickens's fourth paragraph describes the mechanisation of certain branches of cultural activity; just as Carlyle shows that forms of cultural activity which should be 'spiritual and internal' are becoming mechanical and external. Dickens notes that the chapels are 'pious warehouses' – relating the character of religion to the commercial system of society, as Carlyle had done. Education is also singled out for emphasis: 'the M'Choakumchild school was all fact.'

The precise nature of 'hard-fact' education as Carlyle and Dickens conceived it, is analysed in *Hard Times*, especially in Chapters I and II, but at length throughout the whole novel. There you will find a detailed application of these important ideas.

Look at the sentence beginning 'It contained several very large streets' in *Industrialisation and Culture*, p. 380. What do you notice about the rhythm of this sentence?

ANSWER IN MARGIN

SPECIMEN ANSWER

> It's extremely monotonous. The grammatical structure of each clause is similar, or even identical, to that of all the others. The effect of this is to give an effect of tired boredom and oppressive monotony.

This point of language gives us the main difference between a *creative* social critic like Dickens, and one who is primarily concerned with discussion of the political or sociological aspects of a social situation. Dickens is mainly concerned to present or convey the nature of the industrial environment, to give the reader a sense of being actually in it. By the action of reading those sentences we experience the emotional quality Dickens is trying to convey; we participate in the action of the novel. In this passage we are not *told* about boredom, or about what it's like to live in an industrial town, we are *shown*.

Look now at the passage in the fourth paragraph, beginning 'the jail might have been the infirmary'. The construction of this sentence is similar to the one we've discussed. Does it simply attempt to convey the same feeling, or does it make an additional point about the nature of society?

ANSWER IN MARGIN

The rhythm of this sentence really backs up what the sentence is saying, by placing the different buildings within an identical grammatical structure. The syntax breaks down the differences between these institutions, and so provides a strong satirical comment, on the society in which hospital, town hall and prison show no essential differences. If Dickens had written 'The infirmary, the jail and the hospital were all very similar' – it would *mean* the same, but the sentence wouldn't be *saying* the same thing at all.

Now read the extract from Adam Smith's *Wealth of Nations* in *Industrialisation and Culture* H1; and then a passage from John Ruskin's the *Stones of Venice* (1853), which you will find in *Industrialisation and Culture* M3, p. 307. Which sentence in the Ruskin passage pin-points his main objection to the 'division of labour', and what is that objection?

ANSWER IN MARGIN

SPECIMEN ANSWER

'It is not the labour that is divided, but the men.' Ruskin's criticism of the division of labour is quite simple, and expresses the central principles of his social philosophy. He shifts the focus of attention from Adam Smith's emphasis on the pins – on the productive efficiency of the divided system, the increase in the productive power of labour, to the human labourers; who are, in the *Wealth of Nations* reduced to mere shadowy instruments in an industrial machine; and to impersonal factors in an abstract economic theory.

DISCUSSION

To Ruskin, Smith's theory is an example of the 'mechanisation' of important human and social relationships, which is the result of treating men like machines. The opposition to this theory is based on a secularised version of Christian morality, which is radically critical of industrial capitalism and the society it creates. So although Christianity could be (and was) used as a reactionary force to impede social change and to support the existing structure of society, in Ruskin, Christian morality becomes socialism – a radical analysis of industrial society, and a very clearly defined programme for changing and regenerating it.

Look now at this passage from the *Nature of Gothic*:

If you will make a man of the working creature, you cannot make a tool. Let him but begin to imagine, to think, to try to do anything worth doing: and the engine-turned precision is lost at once. Out come all his roughness, all his dullness, all his incapability; shame upon shame, failure after failure, pause after pause: but out comes the whole majesty of him also; and we know the height of it only when we see the clouds settling upon him. And whether the clouds be bright or dark, there will be a transfiguration behind and within them.

Which words or expressions remind you most of Carlyle?

ANSWER IN MARGIN

SPECIMEN ANSWER

'Engine-turned precision'; 'majesty'; 'transfiguration' are the words I would choose. The first phrase makes the contrast, made before Carlyle and Dickens, between the machine and the human being; 'Majesty' is the kind of human attribute Carlyle saw in the Irish 'sanspotatos'; 'transfiguration' is like Carlyle's application of religious vocabulary to secular experience.

DISCUSSION

So Ruskin shares with Carlyle a concept of individual human nature, articulated in religious terms. In this passage the cosmic images of clouds, light and darkness bestow a sense of divine 'majesty' on the individual human being; and the exercise of the *creative* faculty makes possible the experience of 'transfiguration' – the labourer becomes the humanised divinity, the transfigured Christ.

The most significant advance in Ruskin's thinking is his concept of creative work. To the puritan Carlyle all work was valuable; but Ruskin considered that work should be the spontaneous expression of creativity, essential to fullness and richness of life.

In the *Stones of Venice*, Ruskin pointed to Gothic architecture as a form of art which grew out of a healthy social structure; and emphasised its Christian quality, by contrast with the pagan, 'classical' kinds of art and architecture. The mediaeval, Gothic or Christian form of architecture 'recognises the individual value of every soul' because it allows complete freedom for the spontaneous expression of individual creativity. Pagan architecture, on the other hand, insists on the overall perfection of a mathematically-proportioned structure. So the position of the individual labourer in a society which produces the classical kinds of architecture, is analogous to that of the labourer in an industrial system: the whole creative potential is exhausted in making the head of a pin, or in constructing fragments of a building. In each case the demands made on the individual, those of mathematical precision in artistic execution, or of a subordination to a larger mechanical process, are ultimately 'unhumanising'.

Ruskin considered the real malaise of society to be the thwarting of this creativity:

> It is not that men are ill-fed, but that they have no pleasure in the work by which they earn their bread, and therefore look to wealth as the only means of pleasure.

Look at the extract from *Unto this Last* in *Industrialisation and Culture* H11. Where in this passage does Ruskin refer the discussion to a sense of morality, which is suggestive of a religious outlook?

ANSWER IN MARGIN

SPECIMEN ANSWER

> In the distinction between 'political' and 'mercantile' economies.

DISCUSSION

No explicit mention is made here of religion because Ruskin, in arguing with the political economists, confines himself to using their language and their terms of reference. But I think it is clear that in that distinction, Ruskin is substituting an economy based on a sense of morality – referring always to the quality of life for the individual – for an economy which takes no account of human good, but concerns itself mainly with the quickest and most efficient means of getting rich.

The application of Christian morality to individualist economics is really a reversal of emphasis; we should be considering, says Ruskin, not the efficiency of production, and the best way to become a wealthy capitalist, but the whole of society, which must take into account the lives of individuals in every social group. Notice also the importance of *creativity* to the fulfilment of individual lives, and notice especially how broadly Ruskin interprets its meaning – suggesting that the work of the bricklayer and the housewife is as creative as that of the artist.

Read now the extract from *Culture and Anarchy* in *Industrialisation and Culture* H7. What basic point made by Carlyle is repeated here by Arnold?

ANSWER IN MARGIN

SPECIMEN ANSWER

> Arnold repeates Carlyle's argument that things spiritual and internal are becoming 'mechanical' and 'external'. Arnold's criticism in *Culture and Anarchy* is directed mainly towards the materialism of life and thought in the prosperous industrial society of the '60s; and towards new political developments, the organisation of the working class and the extension of the working class and the extension of the franchise created by the 1867 Reform Bill. All these social developments are described as a 'mechanisation' of life.

Which of these two passages is the livelier description? Can you suggest a reason for this?

> The huge demon of mechanism smokes and thunders, panting at his great task, in all sections of English land; changing his shape like a very Proteus; and infallibly, at every change of shape, over-setting whole multitudes of workmen, and as if with the waving of his shadow from afar hurling them asunder, this way and that, in their crowded march and course of work or traffic; so that the wisest no longer knows his whereabout!
>
> *(Carlyle)*

What is freedom but machinery? What is coal but machinery?
What are railroads but machinery? What is wealth but machinery?
What are, even, religious organisations but machinery?

(*Arnold*)

ANSWER IN MARGIN

Fig. 4   Matthew Arnold

SPECIMEN ANSWER

I think the Carlyle passage is clearly more alive than the
Arnold. We'll see why in a moment.

DISCUSSION

Arnold makes substantially the same points as Carlyle and Dickens.
The difference is one of style, and style, as you will see, is far more
than a matter of technical accomplishment and literary artistry – it
is really an essential and important part of what the writer is saying.
Arnold uses the machine metaphor to describe certain developments
in society, but the metaphor is now abstracted from its concrete
basis in the physical machinery, from which we saw it emerge in
Signs of the Times. The close relation between the metaphor and its

origin is clear in the passage from *Chartism* quoted here: Carlyle is really talking about changes in society caused by industrialisation, about the fluctuation of population movements in response to social and economic change, but the metaphor is expressed in concrete terms – in other words, the physical machine is actually there in the metaphor, actively oversetting and hurling people this way and that – as though they were physically caught up in a machine. It's not enough to say that this is merely a vivid and striking way of saying something. For the image of the demon mechanism helps to express the close relationship with the social context, the intimate involvement with industrial society, conveyed by Carlyle's writing.

Carlyle feels a sense of threatening danger in the machine; and he also feels a strongly sympathetic identification with the human beings who are affected by it. What we get from this powerfully-felt perception of social relationships is a sense of involvement – Carlyle and the Irish labourers are in it together.

Arnold has lost the relation between the machine metaphor and its concrete basis. Coal, railroads and wealth are machinery in the metaphorical sense; and that loss of connection expresses a deeper alienation from the industrial environment. Carlyle's insight into individuals enables him to feel into the lives of the Irishmen, whereas Arnold's culture can say: 'Consider these people, then, their way of life, their habits, their manners, the very tones of their voice' – the separation between the writer and society is total.

That careful distancing is the response of a profound alienation. Arnold has lost entirely the sense of a possible structure of social relationships which informs the work of Carlyle, Dickens and Ruskin; his response to industrial society is a retreat into personal relationships; and his concept of culture, the necessary restorative, is largely moulded by class tradition. As soon as Arnold identifies culture with the traditions of Oxford University, we can see how inadequate are his ideas for coping with the industrial society of the nineteenth century.

SECTION 7

INDUSTRIALISM AND PROVINCIAL CULTURE

Most of the writers we have dealt with criticised industrial society from a basis of religious belief in some form or another. There is also an important group of writers whose opposition to industrial progress is based on a cultural allegiance: a strong sense of loyalty to the culture of their upbringing, and a resistance (more or less strong) to the new culture of industrialism which was threatening to change the older traditions. George Eliot, Thomas Hardy, Mark Rutherford, D. H. Lawrence are all examples. Each culture also embodied a strong religious tradition, usually some form of Puritanism: so each writer is concerned, like the other social critics, with a reinterpretation of conventional religion.

George Eliot's allegiance was to the culture of the English Midlands but her provincial sympathies to some extent conflicted with her intellectual position as a free-thinking radical liberal, a leading mind in the intellectual life of the time. Her greatest novel, *Middlemarch* (1870), seems to communicate a strong sense of satisfaction at provincial society's unyielding resistance to change; but her attitudes are by no means simple.

Now read the extract from *Felix Holt* in *Industrialisation and Culture* B1. We are told that provincial society has good and bad points about it. List the main features in each category. The first paragraph of the extract is concerned with scene-setting, sketching a general atmosphere, and doesn't make any concrete statements, so leave it out for the purposes of this question.

GOOD ASPECTS

BAD ASPECTS

SPECIMEN ANSWERS

Your list should look something like this:

GOOD ASPECTS

> 1. The slower pace of life associated with the stagecoach is shown to be richer in experience than the faster pace of modern travel:
>
>   'Posterity may be shot, like a bullet through a tube, by atmospheric pressure from Winchester to Newcastle: that is a fine result to have among our hopes; but the slow old-fashioned way of getting from one end of the country to the other is the better thing to have in the memory.'
>
> 2. The country is described as very beautiful in its profusion of natural growth:
>
>   'Everywhere the bushy hedgerows wasted the land with their straggling beauty', etc.
>
> 3. The description of the 'trim, cheerful villages' in the third paragraph shows country life at its best, provincial culture at its healthiest and most vital.

BAD ASPECTS

> The main point to notice is the *isolation* of provincial culture from much that is important in the life of the country – intellectual culture, politics, religious thinking:
>
> 'The shepherd . . . his glance, accustomed to rest on things very near the earth, seemed to lift itself with difficulty to the coachman. Mail or stagecoach for him belonged to that mysterious distant system of things called "Government", which, whatever it might be, was no business of his. . . .'

DISCUSSION

Felix Holt was written in the context of the 1867 Reform Bill, as part of the general debate about democratisation; so the point about the alienation of people from the system of Government is obviously an important one.

This isolation is an essential feature of the structure of society, and its poor network of communications. The consequences of isolation are described in the passage about the 'small hamlet' which 'seemed to turn its back on the road, and to lie away from everything but its own patch of earth and sky'. George Eliot notes the prevalence of poverty, ignorance and vice – and especially ignorance. It is illiteracy that keeps people out of contact with the influences working in society for social change; influences that are strongly active in the urban society of the industrial town. One of the most important influences is Nonconformist or 'Dissenting' religion, which traditionally associated itself with radical politics. But the inhabitants of the 'small hamlet' are described as safely and securely Protestant, kept so by their ignorance – they know nothing of the techniques of organisation which Nonconformism encouraged, which eventually contributed to the trade unions. 'They were saved from the excesses of Protestantism by not knowing how to read, and by the absence of handlooms and mines to be the pioneers of Dissent: they were kept safely in the *via media* of indifference, and could have registered themselves in the census by a big black mark as members of the Church of England.'

Now look at the description of the manufacturing town. Again, try to appreciate the complexity of attitude by isolating the good and bad points the writer makes about industrial culture.

BAD POINTS

```




```

GOOD POINTS

```




```

SPECIMEN ANSWERS

BAD POINTS

The main argument in this description tries to express the *unnatural* quality of life in the industrial town. The miners with their deformed knees; the handloom weavers and their pale faces, unhealthy from overwork and exhaustion; the women neglecting their children under the pressure of long working hours. Notice also the apocalyptic image of the 'cloudy day and red gloom by night', which recalls the pillars of fire and cloud in 'Exodus'.

The signs of health in the industrial population are the Dissenting chapels, which provide a 'visible sign of religion'; and which (more important) suggest the proximity of political radicalism. 'Here was a population not convinced that old England was as good as possible; here were multitudinous men and women aware that their religion was not the religion of their rulers, who might therefore be better than they were, and who, if better, might alter many things which now made the world perhaps more painful than it need be, and certainly more sinful.'

George Eliot is aware that provincial life combines a valuable social tradition with many social evils. The forces working to remedy those social evils are present in the urban population; but the changes which will improve social conditions will also destroy much that is valuable in the traditional culture of rural society.

EXERCISE

Look now at the passage immediately following the description of the manufacturing town: 'Yet there were the grey steeples too' . . . 'the park and mansion which they shut in from the working-day world.' What point, if any, is George Eliot making here and what would you say about the movement of feeling represented by the transition at 'Yet there were . . .'?

ANSWER IN MARGIN

SPECIMEN ANSWER

The point made is about the isolation and alienation of the aristocracy who live in these 'mansions' which are cut off from the working-day world: they are still the ruling classes, and yet they have no real relationship with the society in which their wealth and influence are so powerful.

As for the movement of feeling, perhaps your response is different, but that transition seems to me a nostalgic sigh for the fineness and dignity of the aristocratic culture which is being threatened by industrialism. This represents a strong allegiance on George Eliot's part that often vitiates her criticism of society.

SECTION 8

AGRICULTURAL LIFE AND THE MACHINE

Now read the extract from *Tess of the d'Urbervilles* in *Industrialisation and Culture* P6, which describes the impact of industrialism on agricultural society. Hardy's response to industrialisation is in some ways similar to George Eliot's. Try to detect the resemblances by answering the following questions.

1. You remember that in *Felix Holt* one of the bad effects of industrialism was shown to be the perversion of the natural rhythms and patterns of life (see p. 33). How does Hardy convey the same point?

2. In *Felix Holt* the lives of the miners and handloom weavers were seen from outside – from the stage-coach window. What is the main difference in Hardy's treatment of his labourers?

SPECIMEN ANSWERS

1. The old men in *Tess* refer back to the days of hand labour, when work was conducted in a more natural manner. The machine, unlike the human labourer, can work indefinitely and without pause: so the human beings who are dependent on it are subjected to excessively long and difficult working hours. This is the 'tyranny' of the machine, which 'keeps up a despotic demand on the endurance of their muscles and nerves'.

2. George Eliot's version is external – she observes without participating. Hardy's observation is dramatised, so the reader is brought much closer to the lives of the labourers, and participates in the action.

DISCUSSION

The external vision is characteristic of George Eliot's presentation of working-class people, who rarely come across in her novels as credible individuals. Hardy dramatises his observation – which means that he vividly describes the scene so it is present to the reader's senses; but it means more than that. The reader experiences the incident in the novel partly through the perceptions of a character, Tess, whom we know as an individual, unlike the observer in the stage-coach in *Felix Holt* (who is, of course, a mere narrative convention). Remember, for example, when Tess notices the neck of the man in front of her, crusted with dirt and husks: the immediacy of the observation identifies us with Tess, brings us closer to the man in front, closer to the machine – we *participate* instead of merely observing. The dramatisation of the action, by the power of the writing, and by the sympathetic identification of reader with central character, brings the reader right into the situation described; conveys more about mechanised labour than many an abstract statement could do.

This contrast is similar to that between Carlyle and Arnold (see p. 58).

3. Again in *Felix Holt*, George Eliot pointed out the lack of relationship between the older agricultural society and the new industrialism. 'Town and country had no pulse in common.' Hardy shows a similar lack of relationship between his labourers and the machine. How does he do it?

4. What sentence gives the reason for this lack of relationship?

SPECIMEN ANSWERS

3. By emphasising the strangeness, the alien character of the machine's attendant: 'The isolation of his manner and colour lent him the appearance of a creature from Tophet, who had strayed into the pellucid smokelessness of this region of yellow grain and pale soil, with which he had nothing in common.'

4. He served fire and smoke; these denizens of the fields served
   vegetation, weather, frost and sun'.

DISCUSSION

The main difference between the two writers is, that George Eliot's
method is *realism* – factual observation, conveyed by a character-
istically external vision. Hardy uses imagery when he compares the
attendant with a 'creature from Tophet', a method which is artistic-
ally more powerful than factual realism. The machine brings an
alien quality of life to the agricultural community by importing new
methods of labour. The natural rhythms and patterns of rural
life – governed by 'vegetation, frost and sun' – the rhythms of the
seasons and the patterns of organic growth – are replaced by the
unnatural rhythms of the machine; which tend to pervert life into
unnatural patterns of experience. Hardy's account is in some ways
more powerful than George Eliot's – on the other hand it is
intellectually simpler – showing only the bad effects of industrialisation.

D. H. Lawrence restored to the tradition of social criticism,
that we have been tracing, its original religious character. Read the
extract from *Twilight in Italy* in *Industrialisation and Culture* P16,
noticing especially the use of religious vocabulary. Can you see
any connection with Carlyle's secularisation of Christianity?

SPECIMEN ANSWER   **ANSWER IN MARGIN**

> The religious spirit is very strong and instinctive in the
> peasant culture: the sense that life is God-given, 'The earth is
> the Lord's and the fullness thereof'. But Paolo also finds
> religious experience in social relationships – see the passage
> on 'his life was a ritual'.

DISCUSSION

The religious consciousness is, most of all, what gives value to the
life of the peasants, which is clearly seen as a life of poverty and
deprivation. Lawrence has an honest and direct perception of this
poverty and its effects on people – notice how he dramatises the
sense of shame which comes from consciousness of poverty, in the
incident of the bread and the fowls. He is aware of the powerful
economic pressures operating on the peasants, persuading them to
change their way of life – to leave Italy and make money in the
industrial society of America. Hardy's engineer, you remember,
was a traveller; his itinerant nature contrasted with the stationary
life of the labourers, who would probably remain in one place all
their lives. Where does Lawrence make a similar point? Underline
or note in the margin the relevant sentences.

SPECIMEN ANSWER

> 'She (Maria) had been in service, and eaten bread and drunk coffee, and known the flux and variable chance of life. She had departed from the old static conception. . . . She did not want her sons to be peasants, fixed and static as posts driven into the earth. She wanted them to be in the great flux of life in the midst of all possibilities.'

DISCUSSION

The 'possibilities' of the new life are perceived here as an attractive, exciting prospect. And of course for the labourer, life can be materially richer and more satisfying in an industrial society than in an agricultural, peasant society.

But Lawrence is also conscious that the break-up of the peasant society involves great losses, in the quality of life. Which is the most important aspect of their lives likely to be lost in the break-up of traditional culture?

ANSWER IN MARGIN

SPECIMEN ANSWER

> The religious consciousness. Paolo instinctively conceives life in a religious way: his life is the expression of worship, unchanged by material circumstances. In industrial society the religious conception will be lost.

DISCUSSION

Lawrence's account of the peasant society, then, is a complex one. As in George Eliot's description of the Midlands, we are shown the degrading influence of poverty, the powerful impulse to change the established way of life in the need for material prosperity. We are also shown the value of the peasant life in its religious quality, which makes the men happy, satisfied and fulfilled, irrespective of material poverty.

Perhaps we could outline at this point some of the functions of the creative social criticism we have been dealing with. Obviously we do not look in Carlyle or Hardy or Lawrence for a concrete programme of reform, or practical suggestions about how society should be changed, or for the kind of programmatic criticism we find in Marx and Engels. And although the social critics were influential in moulding the attitudes of socialists in Britain to industrialisation, they contributed little to the socialists' industrial policy.

What these social critics provide is an analysis of the effects of the machine, of industrialisation and of certain forms of social organisation on the individual human being. They are also concerned to communicate, by techniques of creative language, the experience of living in an industrial environment. We have examined this experience in Dickens and Hardy, but the novelists are not alone in trying to convey the experience: Carlyle and Ruskin do the same thing and by quite similar methods. The creative intention is not only to present the experience to the reader but to engage him, to secure his participation, in the action of the writing.

Creative writing is far too complex a thing to be confined by any single political ideology and I myself believe this to be an advantage: creative art deals with a sense of possibilities, an awareness of the things political thinking tends to leave out. So the critics in this section should not be measured by a criterion of practical effectiveness. Often the most interesting social criticism of this kind is the most complex, the least committed. The last passage we have to examine is probably the most complex one we have seen; it certainly comes to no concrete conclusion and makes no positive or practical suggestions. Whether these facts reduce its essential value is for you to decide.

EPILOGUE: THE DISAPPEARANCE OF RELIGION

So far we have been dealing with religion in its function as an important source of ideas in nineteenth-century social criticism. We have seen that, while the writers' responses to social change are moulded initially by their religion, the thinking out of the social criticism becomes a radical reinterpretation of conventional religion. As the century progressed, the influences which were eroding the foundations of Christianity strengthened, and the alienation of people from conventional religion increased, until it was possible for George Bernard Shaw to base his intellectual system on a total rejection of Christianity. In some ways this rejection really represents the mental liberation it was felt, at the time, to be; in other ways, it represents a significant impoverishment, in breaking away from a vital tradition of ideas, feelings, perceptions of relationship, which had enriched the thought of Carlyle, Dickens and Ruskin.

Shaw was further away from Christianity than any of the writers we have dealt with so far, but at the same time he was intelligent enough to see that religion embodied fundamental and essential human values, and that a rejection of religion committed men to the creation of a new system of values.

EXERCISE

Read through the extract from *Major Barbara* in *Industrialisation and Culture* P12. Imagine yourself to be in Barbara's position in that dialogue, and asking those questions. What would you think of Undershaft's replies?

SPECIMEN ANSWER

> Undershaft's replies are evasions rather than answers. He never takes Barbara's words at their intended valuation, which is of course a Christian one: instead he translates the religious words into more limited meanings.

DISCUSSION

One example of this kind of 'translation' comes at the beginning of the extract, when Barbara gives a moving account of the loss of religious faith, and Undershaft replies by equating religion with machinery, imagining that belief, like machinery is expendable and replaceable. In Undershaft's attitudes the mechanisation of the mind – Carlyle's sense of men becoming 'mechanical in head and heart' has become an extreme position.

EXERCISE

What examples can you find of conventional religious vocabulary and concepts being translated into non-religious meanings? Copy out the words.

Fig. 5 Bernard Shaw campaigning for Keir Hardie (left) in 1910.

SPECIMEN ANSWER

There are several: for example *power* (pp. 417–18) where the traditional 'power' of God is contrasted with the physical power of man-made armaments. The contrast is expanded towards the end (p. 423). Other examples are *soul, sins, salvation*.

EXERCISE

Look carefully now at Shaw's treatment of these three words – *soul, sins, salvation*. In each case he evokes two meanings, and shows the failure of communication between them. Try to explain, with reference to each word:

1. Barbara's meaning.

2. The significance of Undershaft's explanation.

SOUL

1.

2.

SINS

1.

2.

SALVATION

1.

2.

SPECIMEN ANSWERS

In each case you should have found it easy to explain Undershaft's meanings and rather more difficult to talk about Barbara's. The reason for this is the key to the meaning of the dialogue.

SOUL

1. Barbara's use of the word refers of course to a traditional religious concept – but how would we define, or even explain it? The ordinary system of logical explanation simply doesn't help us.

70

2. To Undershaft, saving a person's soul is simply the amending of all his material circumstances – ensuring that he has proper housing, clothing, food.

SINS

1. *Sins* is a bit easier: we can refer back to a traditional system of prescriptive morality like the Ten Commandments, and be fairly clear about what we mean in practice. So Barbara's use presents no problem.

2. Undershaft sees sins as social abuses – in other words, he sees human evil as a consequence of the material environment.

SALVATION

1. *Salvation* in Barbara's terms probably stopped you altogether. Salvation is a state of religious experience completely indefinable in logical terms.

2. Undershaft's version of *salvation* goes with his concept of the soul: all he sees are the material needs of a human being, and his *salvation* is the satisfying of those material needs.

DISCUSSION

So now the reasons for the failure of communication in the dialogue begin to emerge; and also the reason why Undershaft appears to have the better of the argument, though the dialogue doesn't end with a definitive statement from one side or the other. Undershaft's side of the argument is more easily *arguable*. Rational logic is the instrument of his philosophy, and all his statements are verifiable by reference to self-evident facts. Cleanliness, respectability, model homes, good wages and a reasonable standard of living are all facts, presentable, to be seen and touched. Barbara's side of the argument is composed of feelings, emotional and religious convictions, which simply can't be articulated in Undershaft's terms.

Undershaft's arguments are in a sense true, and very important, but essentially limited. Of course it is hypocrisy to talk of religion and morality in the context of a life of suffering and misery caused by purely social evils. But, important as it is, it really doesn't take us far enough.

Look again at the passage (pp. 418–19) about the loss of faith. Which of the two characters are you most disposed to sympathise with?

My own response is to sympathise with Barbara. Her account of the experience is a moving one, mainly because of the metaphor of the earthquake, by which her feelings are conveyed to us through a vivid sensuous impression. Undershaft's logic is really quite acceptable on an intellectual level; and we have no doubt that he's genuinely concerned with human good – in a limited way. But in this reply to Barbara he shows himself insensitive to the profoundest human feelings.

We don't have to accept the Salvation Army's – or any – theological conception of the soul to recognise, as Shaw wants us to recognise, the limitations of Undershaft's position. Barbara knows that there is something else, something other than material reality, but she is unable to articulate it, and, under the impact of Undershaft's rationalist criticism, her religious vocabulary fails her meaning. Her questions are the questions asked by all the social critics of the later nineteenth century, who saw the beneficial effects of the mature industrial state – with its apparatus of democratic government, state intervention and working-class organisation – apparently irrefutably proved. Despite our material amelioration, are we essentially any better? Has life, in the individual and the community, been essentially improved by mechanical efficiency? Granted that it is possible to perfect the external environment, where do we go from there? And of course the questions are still being asked.

ACKNOWLEDGEMENTS

Grateful acknowledgement is made to the following sources for material used in this unit:

TEXT
Heinemann Limited for H. G. Wells, *The Time Machine*; Lawrence & Wishart Ltd. for K. Marx, *Critique of Political Economy*, M. Dobb (ed.).

ILLUSTRATIONS
Glasgow Museums and Art Galleries for Cover; Mansell Collection for Figs. 1, 2 and 3; National Portrait Gallery and 'Vanity Fair' for Fig. 4; Syndication International for Fig. 5.

Notes

Notes

Notes

Notes

Notes

Notes

Notes

Notes

HUMANITIES: A FOUNDATION COURSE